Praise for *Business Relationships That Last*

"In *Business Relationships That Last*, Ed Wallace captures the immediate need for organizations and individuals to build relationships of integrity and confidence. That trust benefits every aspect of service and will help grow your business and generate superior performance. Ed has it exactly right: intent, character, making and keeping commitments, credibility and authenticity — all are invaluable drivers of performance and relationship building that can lower expenses, speed up production, and tear down the barriers preserving market status quo."
  — *Stephen M. R. Covey, author of the* New York Times *bestseller*
    The Speed of Trust

"Your success in life will be largely determined by who you know and who knows you in a positive way. This book shows you how to achieve your personal and professional goals through relationships faster than you ever thought possible."
  — *Brian Tracy, author of* The Power of Charm

"We all know that businesses grow through outstanding relationships. Ed Wallace provides an elegantly simple yet very powerful way to think about and build relationships that last."
  — *Ivan R. Misner, Ph.D.,* New York Times *best-selling author of*
    The 29% Solution

"Ed Wallace provides a compelling and insightful guide on how to grow your business contacts from Acquaintances all the way to Respected Advisors. Differentiate . . . no, distinguish yourself — read this book!"
  — *Linda Kaplan Thaler, CEO, The Kaplan Thaler Group*

"Everything that's not technical is about people. Whether you're already at ease or not comfortable in the relational part of your career, *Business Relationships That Last* will increase your confidence and even your enjoyment in mastering the people skills so critical to achieving your maximum success."
  — *Mark Goulston, Ph.D., author of the* New York Times *bestseller*
    Get Out of Your Own Way at Work

"Those who understand that life is nothing more than a lot of relationships usually are successful. In *Business Relationships That Last,* Ed Wallace provides you with the guidance not only to develop mutually beneficial relationships inside and outside your business but also, more important, to build strong relationships with family, friends, and even adversaries."
  — *Richard Teerlink, CEO (retired), Harley-Davidson, and
    author of* More Than a Motorcycle

"*Business Relationships That Last* captures a whole career's worth of insight and distills it into basic principles that everyone can use to succeed. It actually provides unfair advantage for those in the early stages of their professional lives!"
  — *Chris Malone, Chief Marketing Officer, Choice Hotels*

"I continue to be highly motivated by Ed Wallace's simple yet oh-so-powerful messages on the importance of building strong business relationships. The concepts in *Business Relationships That Last* take the mystery out of relationship building and replace the "secret sauce" with an actionable plan that will help any business professional achieve his/her goals."
  — *David Clary, Senior Vice President, ICG Commerce*

"Ed's been helping Vistage executives outperform their competition through expert workshops on building value through business relationships. Anyone in business (and, quite frankly, outside of it) can gain useful insights from this book's road map for establishing rapport, integrity, trust, and authenticity. From reexamining your sales strategies to staff turnover, this book focuses you on the relationships you need to nurture at each link in your value chain."
  — *Rafael Pastor, Chairman of the Board and CEO, Vistage International*

"Someone once said that wisdom is worth fifty IQ points. There are more than fifty IQ points' worth of wisdom in Ed Wallace's *Business Relationships That Last.* Read it and gain the insights that lie at the heart of all successful business relationships!"
  — *Jeff Westphal, CEO, Vertex Inc.*

"Ed Wallace has done a masterful job in deciphering the holy grail of relationship building, the final piece of the puzzle: How do the few gifted people among us build key relationships that help them achieve their impossible dreams? He has democratized the skill traditionally known to few elite achievers into a process we can all follow."
  — *Razi Imam, CEO and Founder, Landslide Technologies Inc.*

"In a down economy or a good economy, in our personal or our professional lives, relationships are everything. But relationships can't be outsourced. In *Business Relationships That Last*, Wallace takes us to a new level and gives us a framework to take them to outstanding. This is not a must-read for anyone, but for everyone!"

— *Jeff Del Rossa, General Manager, Sales Optimization, Development Dimensions International*

"Most salespeople try to establish relationships intuitively. Ed Wallace's Relational Ladder process shows how to assess and develop relationships on purpose so they can be an integral part of empowering salespeople to achieve at higher levels."

— *John Holland, coauthor of* CustomerCentric® Selling

"*Business Relationships That Last* is an excellent resource that provides guidance, support, and several approaches to move every business relationship strategically from a business Acquaintance to potentially a Professional Peer or possibly a Respected Advisor. We know that businesses grow through relationships, and this book provides the clear direction on how to build ones that last!"

— *Joan Walsh, author of* Ready, Set, Plan, Go! Strategies to Accelerate Your Success *and* Blazing Your Own Trail—A Guide for Women on the Way Up

"In today's fast-moving, global economy, every product or service you provide is being commoditized at warp speed. The only thing in business today that cannot be commoditized is the relationship you have with each of your prospects, colleagues, clients, and partners. Wallace's work is logical, practical, and tactical and will help you conquer the new business world we live in by providing you with an easy-to-use approach to build "business relationships that last." Buy it, read it, and most important, use it!"

— *Peter Winick, Senior Strategist and Consultant*

"Ed Wallace shows us the critical path to improving business performance . . . What is at once game-changing and refreshingly simple, Ed uses down-to-earth stories and charm along with a terrific how-to process to move the dial on results through relational capital."

— *David Henkin, Vice President, Managed Services, Vertex Inc.*

"Our work with the principles and process that Ed Wallace shares in *Business Relationships That Last* has led to a renewed focus on the importance of quality relationships with our key customers in optimizing our business performance."

— *Jim Bounds, CEO, DMC Inc.*

"Every day my relationships pay dividends. It took me twenty years to learn how to develop them; I wish that I had had this book sooner."
  — *Gary Bender, CFO, Abex Inc.*

"For business leaders and sales professionals ready to stop talking about the importance of their relationships and start following a measurable, proven process to improve them, Ed's easy-to-understand and engaging book has the information, process, and implementation tools to get you there — just be sure to read it before your competition does."
  — *Mark Green, President and Founder, Performance Dynamics Group LLC*

"Ed Wallace has hit it out of the park with *Business Relationships That Last*! He has masterfully exposed the myth of "relationship magic" and given us a hands-on, step-by-step guide to leverage the full power of our business relationships to build sustained success, to improve performance, and to generate outstanding results. This could be the biggest competitive differentiator of our times!"
  — *Roxanne Kaufman, President and Founder, ProLaureate*

"Ed captures the essence and process of building great business relationships. His easy style and warmth underlie a rigorous and real method and philosophy for establishing, cultivating, and leveraging the key contacts we all make in business and life. Ed's five steps are game-changers and essential for any business leader."
  — *Jose Palomino, President, Value Prop Interactive*

"In the post-meltdown economy, excellent business relationships are moving from optional to essential. Ed Wallace's insightful and enjoyable guide is a great starting point to help managers weave relationship cultivation into the fabric of their companies."
  — *Norman Myers, Chairman, Relationship Networking Industry Association*

BUSINESS
RELATIONSHIPS
THAT
LAST

5 STEPS TO
TRANSFORM
CONTACTS
INTO HIGH
PERFORMING
RELATIONSHIPS

ED WALLACE

Foreword by **RONALD M. SHAPIRO**, *New York Times* best-selling author

GREENLEAF
BOOK GROUP PRESS

Published by Greenleaf Book Group Press
Austin, TX
www.greenleafbookgroup.com

Distributed by Greenleaf Book Group LLC

For ordering information or special discounts for bulk purchases, please contact Greenleaf Book Group LLC at PO Box 91869, Austin, TX 78709, 512.891.6100.

Design and composition by Greenleaf Book Group LLC
Cover design by Greenleaf Book Group LLC

Publisher's Cataloging-In-Publication Data
(Prepared by The Donohue Group, Inc.)

Wallace, Ed, 1959–
  Business relationships that last : 5 steps to transform contacts into high-performing relationships / Ed Wallace ; foreword by Ronald M. Shapiro. -- 1st ed.

  p. : ill. ; cm.

  Includes bibliographical references and index.
  ISBN: 978-1-60832-001-1

1. Social networks. 2. Strategic alliances (Business) 3. Success in business.
I. Shapiro, Ronald M. II. Title.

HF5386 .W25 2009
650.13   2009928415

Part of the Tree Neutral™ program, which offsets the number of trees consumed in the production and printing of this book by taking proactive steps, such as planting trees in direct proportion to the number of trees used: www.treeneutral.com

TreeNeutral

Printed in the United States of America on acid-free paper

13 12 11 10 09   10 9 8 7 6 5 4 3 2 1

First Edition

To Laurie, Brett, and Grant — with whom I have my

most important and cherished relationships

Contents

PART II: THE 5 STEPS TO TRANSFORM CONTACTS INTO HIGH-PERFORMING RELATIONSHIPS

PART III: ACTION PLANNING

Foreword

Not long ago, as I was recovering from an extensive tour for my last book, I began sketching out a plan for my next one. I had already chosen as its subject my core philosophy for doing business and, for that matter, enjoying life: building and maintaining meaningful relationships.

The premise for my proposed relationships book was a systematic approach that businesspeople of any ilk could pursue to build their own meaningful relationships. Today, I have forsaken that book! It has already been written, with grace and insight, by Ed Wallace with his book: *Business Relationships That Last*.

Using lessons learned from a taxi driver named Max and experiences in an array of business contexts, Ed shapes a philosophy and approach to building relationships that is both learnable and workable. He lays out values and a plan directed at helping all of us achieve what Max did in turning his ostensibly simple transactional taxi business into one of strong and rewarding personal relationships.

Not everyone has the good fortune to observe and learn firsthand from their own "Max." People like him are very rare. Luckily, Ed had the wisdom to capture Max's advice and philosophy and to organize them into a repeatable system. Ed also draws on other business executives with whom he has dealt to illustrate and enliven his method.

When reading *Business Relationships That Last*, you will be reminded of some things you always knew, but you will learn to use those same ideas in a new and focused way. By providing "five steps to transform contacts into high-performing relationships," as well as insight into the three essential components of relational capital — credibility, integrity, and authenticity — Ed also gives you a road map for moving your relationships from the transactional level into sustained lifelong partnerships. By making his own life the canvas for portraying this journey, Ed vividly proves that little things make a big difference.

The author believes, and makes very clear on the page, that business isn't just business, it's personal. And he's right. You have to recognize that the transactional aspects of your relationship — arriving on time with a product or service that has value, having a well-prepared professional presentation — are easily achieved by anyone who is motivated to sell. The difference lies with your willingness and ability to be present in the moment and to do all the little things that reflect the intangible qualities of "becoming a person people want to do business with."

People are sizing you up in every business interaction, intuitively and decisively determining whether you are worthy of their interest, trust, and money. In Max's case, it was his ability to listen and to find the real value in the relationship, and then using that information to advance the personal relationship with Ed and his other customers, that really made the difference.

As any good business book would advise, the power behind relational capital does not stop once you hang your "business hat" at the door. The methods and skills that Ed prescribes in these pages will help you build better, stronger, and more rewarding relationships with your friends, family, and even casual acquaintances. As you read Ed's words, be honest with yourself. Are you really getting the most out of your relationships? Are you constantly putting out fires and having to "re-sell" yourself, your ideas, and your products or services? Or are you presenting yourself as a credible and reliable person upon whom your transactional partner will want to rely again and again?

Ed's five steps, along with the other key elements of relational capital cited in this terrific book, will aid any businessperson's efforts to become better. But the real bang for your buck here comes with how the book helps you become a better partner in any relationship. If, on the other hand, you resist following Ed's system, then remember Harry Truman's immortal words: "It's what you learn after you know it all that really counts."

Ronald M. Shapiro
Chairman, Shapiro Negotiations Institute
Baltimore, Maryland
www.shapironegotiations.com

Acknowledgments

Thanks to my truly great colleagues and friends for their amazing efforts in support of bringing forth *Business Relationships That Last*:

My mother, Connie, and my sister, Jennifer, your love and commitment are an everlasting inspiration.

Jim Mullen, my true Respected Advisor and the best business partner imaginable, your support while I completed this latest journey with Max will never be forgotten.

Chris Malone, friendship knows no bounds, and I am so fortunate to call you my friend.

Paul Wesman, here's to our third book! Your magic is as powerful as ever.

Bill Crawford, Jay Hodges, and Linda O'Doughda, you are the most patient miracle workers I will ever know.

The Greenleaf Book Group team, your belief and confidence in this project were unwavering.

Gary Bender, your belief in Max and Friday afternoon check-in calls will always be treasured.

Jose Palomino, you're just plain brilliant, and I'm blessed to have such a great friend living right next door.

David Henkin, the most balanced man on earth and my "state of being" guru.

Peter Winick, your "challenges" continue to push me and bring extraordinary value to my world.

Roxanne Kaufman, I wish I could bottle your energy and enthusiasm for every undertaking and share them with the world.

Jon Sappey and Jim Bounds, everyone needs a first client, and we could not have been luckier.

Mark Jankowski and all of my friends from Shapiro Negotiations Institute, for your belief in the power of relationships.

Chris Kiminas — and all of my friends at Landslide — thank you for making relational capital *digital*.

Jim Lucas and my friends from Vistage International, your coaching and support are like vitamin C in my life.

Jeff Westphal, as we head into the next phase of our lives and careers, I know I can always count on our Respected Advisor relationship.

Jerry Block, your help with perspective on the manuscript was priceless.

Jason and Kim Coleman from Stranger Studios, your ongoing support of all of my firm's business and creative needs is truly valued.

My friends from the Gryphon Café and Burlap and Bean Café, I appreciate the wonderfully creative environment you shared as I developed this book.

Introduction

We all instinctively know that relationships are *the* key to business success. In fact, I recently learned that 88 percent of executives view the strength of customer and client relationships as the main reason why they achieve their revenue goals each year. This reality is reaffirmed when we think about the successful businesspeople we know: an attribute they all share is the ability to develop outstanding business relationships.

It's ironic then that despite spending millions of dollars to devise strategic plans to achieve desired results, only 24 percent of corporations formally *track* the relational aspects of their client and prospect interactions within their CRM (customer relationship management) systems. In fact, less than 5 percent actually focus on *advancing* business relationships as a strategy for achieving their forecasts and quotas. Far too little attention is given to intentionally creating relational capital, the distinctive value created by people in a business relationship. Unaware that creating relational capital is a process that can be learned and measured, we often leave the idea of advancing our most important business relationships to chance.

I recall an executive mentioning to me that, at times, growing a business relationship is like trying to hold onto sand as it slips between your fingers. Reading this book will help everyone in sales and other client-facing positions within an organization learn transformational skills, perspectives, and strategies they can apply immediately to build and strengthen their business relationships — in essence, a way to cup their hands to hold onto the dynamic relational sand. I like using the term *client-facing* to describe all businesspeople who have frequent contact with customers that use their products and services: this includes professionals in sales, business development, account management, marketing, customer service, and consulting, the CEO, the CFO, executive administrative assistants, and — sometimes most important — the receptionist. In other words, just about everyone in a business! I believe that despite their levels or formal roles these professionals are ambassadors for every organization's brand and client relationships.

> Relational capital is the distinctive value created by people in a business relationship.

If you're like many of my clients and the professionals who attend my workshops, reading this book will be the first time you've thought about achieving your goals through a focused, intentional approach to advancing your business relationships. It's a new way to reach your goals, and you'll see immediate results. As you read, you'll specifically learn how to:

- Achieve your quotas and goals by identifying, measuring, and proactively advancing your most important business relationships

- Internalize a five-step process for advancing each business relationship, transforming your business *Acquaintances* into *Professional Peers* and, ultimately, *Respected Advisors*

- Launch new business relationships with confidence and ease
- Understand how your customers' Relational GPS—their goals, passions, and struggles—will help you create business relationships that last
- Develop an Action Plan that allows you to apply what you learned to your existing client opportunities

The reason I wrote *Business Relationships That Last* was to share with you the five-step approach that thousands of professionals—including Fortune 2000 senior executives, business owners, salespeople, and partners in major corporations and professional service firms—have learned, internalized, and implemented in their businesses. I've based this book on the "Creating Relational Capital" learning series of workshops that my firm produces and delivers to our corporate clients. I've expanded many of those ideas to create this practical guide that will help you immediately start to build outstanding business relationships.

How to Use This Book

Business Relationships That Last is divided into three parts. Part 1, "What Is Relational Capital?" introduces my friend Max and how I learned about the "principle of worthy intent" and the foundational philosophy for creating relational capital by observing the way he turned a commodity business into a remarkable customer experience. This section also develops the essential qualities of relational capital and introduces the five steps of what I call the Relational Ladder process to transform your contacts into high-performing relationships.

Part 2, "The 5 Steps to Transform Contacts into High-Performing Relationships," helps you learn and internalize that five-step process to distinguish yourself with every customer and business contact. You will understand how to use the five steps to advance your business relationships in support of achieving your quotas and specific objectives. Also throughout part 2, I include Action Points, which are relevant suggestions that prompt you to apply the ideas you've just read so that you can internalize specific skills. Of course, Max makes his presence known through stories in these chapters, alongside anecdotes from other business leaders.

Part 3, "Action Planning," explains your "relational intelligence" (RQ) and gives you the opportunity to take the web-based RQ Assessment that will help you measure the value of your relational capital for your five most important business relationships. You will also connect the learning to your own work as you develop an Action Plan in support of your next twelve months' goals. I share seven "relational reinforcers" to help you immediately apply the new learning to the strategies developed in your Action Plan, which will lead you to a level I call "sustained relational fluency." Finally, I explain the impact relational capital gains will have on your most important business relationships.

Chapters 1 through 11 conclude with a section called "Relational Insights" that emphasizes the key points in the chapter for recall and future reference.

My hope is that you will enjoy learning how easy and how rewarding it is to build business relationships that last.

PART ONE

What Is Relational Capital?

Chapter 1

It's the Little Extras!

Little things make big things happen.
—John Wooden

Imagine that today is the last day of your sales cycle and you still have not made your monthly quota. This scenario was all too often a reality for me during my early years in sales. Now imagine that you have built such outstanding business relationships that you could contact any number of your clients and ask for their help with your quota shortfall. Imagine a level of mutual trust and commitment so deep that this request will be as easy for you to make as it will be for your clients to understand. And, finally, imagine they not only understand your need but also offer to fulfill it by signing a contract or placing an order earlier than they had planned.

My passionate belief after a twenty-five-year career in sales, executive leadership, and now business ownership is that creating business relationships that last is *the* secret to success. As I reflect on all of the amazing technological advances that have evolved during this time, from communicating via the World Wide Web to staying connected through our BlackBerry devices, I find one remarkable, simple constant: *business is still driven by people and relationships.*

Eventually, human beings need to interact with one another in order to work through all of the details associated with their organizations doing business together. Whether it be the use of a product or service or the acquisition of a new business, humans— with all of our knowledge, skills, goals, emotions, biases, and fears—need to collaborate to get things accomplished.

> Even in the midst of technological advances I find one remarkable, simple constant: *business is still driven by people and relationships.*

Developing business relationships that last with your clients sometimes seems like a lot of extra work, especially if you cannot ensure a predictable return on the investment from all of your efforts. I mentioned in the introduction that advancing such relationships can be like trying to hold on to sand at the beach; inevitably, it runs between your fingers. But even though lasting business relationships can seem as elusive as holding on to sand, learning and applying a process to help you "cup them in your hands" makes it much less challenging than you might think. To illustrate that point, I want to share with you a story about my friend Max, the greatest developer of business relationships I have ever known. Listen and learn from Max just how easy and natural developing quality client relationships can be.

Max

A number of years ago, my sales efforts required that I travel a great deal. I didn't like being away from my family any more than necessary, so I became king of the day-trippers. It got so that I could leave my home on the East Coast around 5:00 a.m. for a meeting in Minneapolis or Des Moines and still make it back home the same day for a late dinner and to see Brett, our first child, for a few precious minutes before tucking him into bed.

The night before one of these trips, my car developed an engine problem. I asked my wife, Laurie, to reserve a taxi to the airport for me. As usual, when she got involved in helping me solve one of my problems, remarkable events began to unfold.

The next morning I waited anxiously for the car to arrive. At precisely 5:00 a.m. I noticed an old-fashioned British taxi, with stately, rounded exterior lines, running boards, and a large passenger compartment pull up in the front of the house. Even in the faint light of dawn I could tell the car was spotlessly clean.

In the short amount of time it took me to exit the house and lock the door, the driver had already exited the taxi and was on his way up the walk toward the house. He was a tall, lanky fellow with glasses and the sort of calm, kind face you might see in a Norman Rockwell painting. I was about to learn that he was not your average taxi driver.

He gave me a warm, "Good morning," and we walked together toward his parked taxi. I climbed into the passenger area of the car, settled into a luxurious leather seat, stretched out my legs, and felt a deep sense of comfort and relief. When the driver started the car, I noticed there was no noise — no scratchy dispatcher's voice barking instructions, no jangling music on the radio. A cooler within reach provided a supply of bottled water. It was amazing!

As we pulled away, the driver turned around to introduce himself. "Hello, Ed, my name is Max," he said with a smile.

"Glad to meet you, Max," I replied, wondering how he knew my name.

As we drove, he asked me a couple of questions about myself. Since I'm pretty much my own favorite topic, I happily offered plenty of information. He was a terrific listener, and I found myself sharing a good deal about my life with this person that I hardly knew. He had a special calm, sincere demeanor that made me feel comfortable opening up to him. He took special note when I told him about our new young son and how he had just started sleeping through the night.

When we arrived at the airport, I gave Max a more generous tip than I usually give drivers. I had so thoroughly enjoyed his company and the stress-free ride to the airport I asked him to schedule me for the following Tuesday.

Max hesitated and then said, "I'm truly sorry, Ed, but I cannot pick you up next week."

"What's wrong, Max, is it something I said?" I inquired, half-jokingly.

"No, nothing like that, Ed. I just have a great deal of fares—friends, that is—and they usually need to book three to four weeks in advance with me."

"For a ride to the airport at five o'clock in the morning?" I asked incredulously.

"Yes, I have a lot of friends," Max responded. "I just happened to have a cancellation last night before I got your wife's request for a ride."

"Okay, how about three weeks from today?" I tried again.

"That works. I look forward to seeing you then," Max answered, and he was off.

Three weeks later, on the morning Max had agreed to pick me up, I was running a few minutes behind schedule. I kept checking out the front window, hoping to catch him before he rang the door-bell. At exactly 5:00 a.m., I heard a gentle tap on the screen door. As I walked to the taxi with Max, I imagined how many people had probably ridden in his taxi over the previous three weeks, yet despite that large number, he had remembered I had an infant son who was most likely sleeping at such an early hour. Max's thoughtfulness and ability to remember details about my life impressed me.

During my next several rides to the airport in Max's marvelous taxi, we talked almost entirely about my life. (Notice that I was no longer driving myself to the airport!) He asked about my work, where I was traveling to, my ambitions, my family. I could hardly believe how at ease I felt opening up to him. I was more comfortable telling Max things about myself than I was telling people I had known much longer.

The more time I spent with Max, the more interested I became in learning how he was able to make me — and most likely all of his customers — feel so comfortable. When asked, he told me a few things about himself, his business, and his day-to-day schedule as a taxi driver and small business owner.

His clients could not be easily categorized. They were local CEOs and their colleagues. They were sales professionals going to the airport and elderly people going shopping. They were groups of ladies going to the city for a day at the art museum, lunch, and a nice tour of the historic district.

> "It's the little extras that turn fares into friends."

I finally asked how he had developed such a long list of loyal customers, hoping he would provide me with a "secret to success" that most client-facing professionals dream about.

"Simple, Ed," he answered, holding his thumb and index finger about an inch apart. "It's the little extras that turn fares into friends."

I thought about what Max meant by the "little extras." Sure, it was great fun riding around in his taxi; it was the only one of its kind in the area and attracted a lot of attention. But that was only a small part of what made Max a success — and he *was* a remarkable business success.

After a few minutes, I realized that his entire business philosophy was based on friendship, and the little extras that friends would do for each other. So I asked, "What are these little extras? Are they the on-time arrivals? The courtesy and warmth? Treating everyone equally? The impeccable upkeep of the taxi and the quiet environment it provides? The bottled water? Listening, remembering, and having a genuine interest in the riders' lives? The gentle tap on the screen door at five o'clock in the morning?"

Max answered, "Yes."

"Which one?" I asked. Just as the words were coming out of my mouth, I got it. Of course, how could I not get it? Max was skilled at identifying and aligning with each rider's specific needs and situation. But how did he do this?

I believe that Max woke up every morning thinking not that he was going to work but that he was going to spend the day with his close friends. This is obviously a very different approach from viewing business as a series of transactions in which both parties want something from each other. If we define *friends* as "parties who *help* one another," and if you consider everyone you interact with your friend, then adding the *little extras* in your business relationships would be as easy as including them in your personal life, which you do naturally.

On the simplest level, Max's job was to provide a ride from one place to another. Any driver could do that, and do it on time, safely, and courteously. But when you rode with Max, the quality of the relationship, the conversation — the whole experience — was so enjoyable, supportive, enlightening, and pleasant that you didn't want the trip to be over. He had mastered the art of taking his so-called simple business from a merely transactional level to the level of high-value personal relationships, to creating a memorable experience between human beings.

I had the good fortune to travel with Max for almost four years, and during those years I began to see how poorly I was managing my own business relationships. The most important perspective I learned from him was that if I lose sight of the fact that I am dealing with a *real person* — for instance, the real person on the other end of a call or an e-mail — then I miss the opportunity to enrich my business endeavors and life with the growth and learning that comes from true interaction with others. Many people have taken the notion of work-life balance to mean that you only need to focus on relationships in the "life," or personal, part of that equation. But as my early travels with Max illustrate, there is tremendous gain to be had from treating your business relationships with as much care.

The Principle of Worthy Intent

In writing this book and working with my own clients to advance their key business relationships, I reflected on Max's philosophy about the little extras and my own experiences throughout my career. Whether I call it relational capital — which I defined as "the distinctive value created by people in a business relationship" — or "the little extras" — as Max liked to say — there is one overarching principle that drives ultimate success when working with clients. I call this the principle of worthy intent, which is the inherent promise you make to keep the

> The principle of worthy intent is the inherent promise you make to keep the other person's best interests at the core of your business relationship.

other person's best interests at the core of your business relationship.

Keeping the client's best interest as your focus is the golden rule for client-facing professionals. This realization has stood the test of time as I advanced through my career from an inside sales rep to an executive, and it remains just as important for me now as a business owner. Those little extras that I connected to Max transformed his transactional *activities* (maintaining an impeccable taxicab and asking questions) into the *relational attributes* (such as listening and remembering) that really defined him and set him apart.

Max's relational attributes emerged through the way he internalized and responded to what I call his riders' Relational GPS— their goals, passions, and struggles. I develop the Relational GPS concept in greater detail later in this book; for now let me point out that Max understood that "asking questions" was important, but the way he processed and responded to the information his clients provided was the secret to his success.

Figure 1.1 depicts the transformation of a few of Max's transactional activities to the relational attributes that his clients attached to him and the experience of riding in his taxi.

Transactional activities can be provided to some degree by anyone in the taxi business, but relational attributes are powerful and lasting, although harder to develop. Relational attributes create business relationships that last because clients ascribe to you qualities that distinguish you among your competitors. The word *differentiate* has been used for quite some time to describe the way in which you set yourself apart from your competition. It's actually been overused to the point that it has now become a "commodity" to many. Plus, differentiating is not always clearly a positive description. Conversely, relational attributes create a "distinctive value"—not merely a differentiation. This distinctive

Figure 1.1: Max's Relational Attributes

Transactional Activities	Relational Attributes
Impeccable taxicab	Respecting riders' needs
On-time arrivals	Respecting riders' time
Asking questions	Listening and remembering
Talking	Sharing relevant information
Scheduling	Keeping commitments

value begins with your "worthy intent" toward your client's goals, passions, and struggles, and it sets you on the path to advancing your business relationships in a way that leads to your ultimate success in today's non-differentiable business environment. Relational attributes create the "distinctive value" that is reflected in the definition of relational capital.

Whether you are in your taxi or at work with your clients, the little extras make all the difference.

RELATIONAL INSIGHTS

☑ Despite the pace of technology and innovation, business is still driven by people and relationships.

☑ Relational capital is the distinctive value created by people in a business relationship.

☑ The principle of worthy intent is the inherent promise you make to keep the other person's best interests at the core of your business relationship.

☑ Transactional activities, such as having an impeccable taxicab and arriving on time, can be easily duplicated and commoditized; the result is that less value is conveyed and business relationships are shorter term.

☑ Relational attributes like Max's ability to listen and remember personal details about his fares are distinguishable and transform a service offering into an enjoyable, more valuable experience between people.

Chapter 2

Success Is Not a Secret

My business is built on relationships!
—The CEO of most major corporations

Just about every Fortune 2000 executive and business owner I have met or worked with tells me flat out that his or her business is built on relationships. We all believe it intuitively, and we all expect to hear this message from other business leaders. Warm and fuzzy statements about customer service, trusted partnerships, and client-driven strategies can be convincing in marketing materials, on websites, in annual reports, and during presentations. And frankly, if these declarations weren't there, we would think something was missing. Run a Google search of the phrase "business built on relationships" and you'll get more than three million hits! If that isn't a testament to the ubiquity of this kind of conviction, I don't know what is.

A recent survey of CEOs and sales executives conducted by Candice Bennett and Associates Inc., an independent market research firm, found that 88 percent of executives believe that the strength of customer and client relationships is the main reason why they meet or beat their revenue goals every year. So why is it that when I ask these same senior executives and business owners how they are consciously investing in the skills and processes needed to nurture and advance these important business relationships, most are surprised by the concept? In fact, research indicates that merely one out of every four corporations formally *tracks* the relational aspects of its sales processes in support of its plans. It's no surprise then that formally investing in the organization's business relationships does not specifically appear on most corporate scorecards.

Many of these business leaders view developing business relationships as an instinctive mind-set rather than as an approach based on beliefs, new skills, and a repeatable process. I've actually heard the phrase "We focus on hiring people with the most magic" from many business leaders who honestly believe this. They let these "magicians" work with clients, all the while hoping some of the magic rubs off on the other folks in the office.

As business professionals, we all know the buzz about investment capital, intellectual capital, and even human capital. But relational capital may be the most undervalued, least understood, most ignored – yet the *most important* – asset in your company and in your own portfolio. And while as business practitioners we've remained unfamiliar with this concept of creating relational capital, academics have been paying more attention to the subject in recent years.

For example, researchers have quantified the impact of a focused investment in business relationships on business performance. Their findings have been remarkable. A study conducted in 2007 by Dr. Theresa Welbourne of the University of Michigan Ross School of Business, in partnership with the staffing firm Adecco North America and the measurement consultancy eePulse, identified relational capital as *the* prevailing competitive advantage for large companies. (The complete white paper, titled "The Intrinsic Link Between Human and Relational Capital," is available through the Knowledge Center link on the website www.relationalcapitalgroup.com.)

And at the October 2007 World Business Forum—a global organization that brings business leaders together to collaborate on key commercial and industrial issues—the importance of business relationships was the central theme. Pamela Babcock highlighted this in an e-article (covering the forum titled: "'Relational Capital' Becomes Newest Differentiator of Competitiveness"). "Strong relationships that employees have with the people they serve in and outside the organization, along with high employee engagement levels and the willingness to go above and beyond expectations, aren't easy for competitors to replicate, and [these relationships] directly impact the organization's performance." This entire conference was another compelling reminder that business relationships prevail as the key driver for better performance.

Because of the fluid nature of business relationships, however, companies continue to struggle with just how to capitalize on this opportunity. Helping them learn how is exactly why I decided to write this book.

The Need for a Plan

After researching and working with more than three hundred client companies, The Relational Capital Group has learned that fewer than one in twenty of these companies actually creates specific strategies for its professionals to use to develop and strengthen the relationships required to achieve its revenue and profit objectives. This leaves a gap, a "relational gap," in the execution of a company's well-planned strategy (see figure 2.1).

Figure 2.1: The Relational Gap

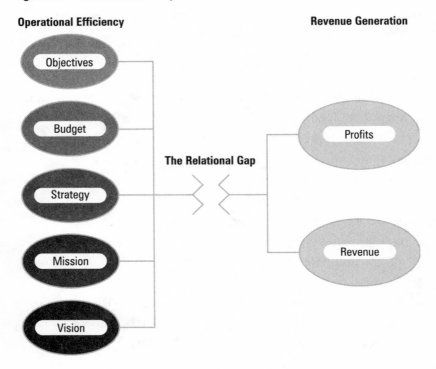

This graphic represents how a company develops a strategy to generate revenue and profit through a series of carefully planned processes. Most often these processes include a company's vision, mission statement, strategic plan, budget, operational plan, and list of objectives. Business leaders have performed quite well on the operations side of their businesses through process improvement, re-engineering, and detailed planning. While this exhibits mastery on the operations side of their businesses, there is little more at this point that leaders can wring from their operational efficiencies. Ultimately, the company must close the gap between all of these operational efficiencies and the need to generate revenue. Strategically planning to develop outstanding business relationships is the way to bridge this relational gap in a highly competitive environment that is already saturated with similar products and services.

No matter how much an organization refines its business relationship with a client, additional steps can always be taken to further develop and strengthen that relationship. Rarely, however, do organizations help their professionals cultivate the skills necessary to take a business relationship to the next level to produce the desired results. When I speak with senior executives about their relationship-cultivation strategies with clients, I frequently hear some variation of the magician theme I spoke of earlier. From this I conclude that the professionals being hired are expected to improvise their way into high-performing client relationships.

> Client-facing professionals being hired today are expected to improvise their way into high-performing client relationships.

According to AskForensics, a sales-growth company that helps Fortune 500 corporations win business and fortify critical accounts, relationships play the *key* role in why sales are won or lost. Recently, AskForensics researchers analyzed $5 billion worth of corporate sales proposals and learned that

- Fifty-two percent of sales are lost because client-facing professionals failed to identify and understand their prospects' requirements
- A sharp relational atrophy takes place during the handoff from sales to account management
- Failures occur with both prospects and clients due to the salespeople's lack of focus and their inability to establish outstanding business relationships with either group

- Without a plan other than to hire "great people," leaders repeatedly risk failing to establish strong client relationships

As Rick Reynolds, president of AskForensics, states: "Clients and prospects don't always articulate their needs. In fact, they may not really know what they need. Their needs surface only after you have developed a strong, trusting relationship with the client."

We all create plans and strategies for many aspects of life: education, careers, building a home, retirement, and even playing tic-tac-toe with our children. So why leave the development of important business relationships largely to improvisation, especially when these relationships will help close the relational gap and advance revenue, profits, and enterprise value?

Even Magicians Have a Plan

To many organizational leaders, business relationships seem abstract, mysterious, and impossible to quantify, especially when compared to planning an acquisition, revamping a compensation system, assessing a sales pipeline, or setting the price for a product. They may consider developing and advancing a business relationship too fluid, too difficult to understand or explain to be cultivated through the use of a plan.

Even if creating solid business relationships did rely on magical spells and charms, however, the process would still require a strategy. A professional magician like David Copperfield may appear to rely on natural talents, but he actually has an intricate *plan* behind every amazing illusion he performs. He does not possess some inherent ability that allows him to improvise magic. In fact, some of his illusions require such strict precision at every step of the process that one slipup could be fatal. Magicians must repeatedly practice each step of any trick until they can perform it flawlessly.

In today's business environment where the margin for error is narrower than ever, business leaders cannot cross their fingers and hope everything will work out when it comes to developing critical, revenue-generating business relationships. Just like all of their other mission-critical business processes, they have to develop a plan and a repeatable process to eliminate the relational gap. Thereafter, they need to ensure that their employees practice following the plan until they achieve the desired results.

The Great Ad-libbers

Whenever I hear the term *ad-lib*, I think of a wonderfully talented quarterback named Randall Cunningham who played for the Philadelphia Eagles during the 1980s. In my opinion (which many real football experts hold also), Randall was the most physically gifted quarterback to ever play professional football. He was at his best when he could rely on his physical talents to single-handedly win a game.

Cunningham played for a coach named Buddy Ryan, who was known as a defensive genius and therefore emphasized that aspect in every game plan. Ryan commented during many interviews that the game plan would focus on the defense and that he just needed Randall "to make a few plays" on offense for the team to win. This approach delivered above-average performance during the regular season, but during his five-year coaching tenure, Ryan never won a play-off game with the talented Cunningham. Needless to say, Ryan did not have his contract renewed. As Philadelphia Eagles fans, my friends and I always wondered how well Randall would have done if he actually had a plan to follow and only had to rely on ad-libbing when it was most needed.

In business, of course, there are those professionals who have a natural ability—like Randall Cunningham's ability on the football field—to create productive relationships. Unfortunately for corporations, the latest research by Sales Benchmarking Index indicates that more than 87 percent of large company sales come from just 13 percent of their salespeople. We all know a handful of these magical *relational rock stars*; they're the folks who develop their business relationships through ad-libbing, instinct, experience, and luck. In most cases, however, relational high performers rarely analyze how they developed their solid relationships, prefer to ad-lib, and are unable to transfer these skills and their approach to others.

So the bottom line is that just as professional football teams need to rely on more than an ad-libbing quarterback, corporations likewise need more sales from all of their client-facing professionals, not just their relational rock stars.

"We All Make Boxes!"

One person who knows the value of getting more sales from all of his client-facing professionals—and so, appropriately, trains his staff to become better at focusing on relational capital—is Jerry, a client and friend who owns a rapidly growing corrugated box–manufacturing business. In a word, Jerry is a true *relational* capitalist!

During a meeting with his sales and management team in which they were discussing the other companies in their industry, Jerry stated, simply, "We all make boxes." He was not speaking metaphorically; he literally meant that all of the companies in the industry make indistinguishable corrugated boxes. He knew that consciously growing their business relationships was required to continue distinguishing themselves among those competitors.

In a discussion about how the competition was suffering through consolidating or was even going out of business, Jerry made it clear that their company was thriving. The success of the company, he claimed, went beyond its technical expertise and the millions of dollars that had been invested in capital, equipment, and technology. Due to the nature of the industry, the opportunities for distinction based on technology and investment were long gone, and the company needed these capabilities and resources just to stay in the game. What Jerry's family-owned company had succeeded in doing for more than sixty years was to build outstanding business relationships, and now the company's continued survival and growth depended on retaining and expanding these relationships.

As Jerry puts it:

> In the packaging business, like most businesses, all our competitors have access to the same manufacturing technology, the same computer technology for processing orders, and the same shipping technology for getting the product to the customers on time. Electronic communications give everyone the same tools to handle customer service and support. So what you are left with to distinguish yourself is the quality of the relationships you build. It's the trust and confidence you establish with clients, the understanding of their unique needs, the responsiveness to every situation. That's what your real brand is today.

To that end, Jerry makes sure that the status and advancement of relationships are included in every sales meeting and every conversation his client-facing professionals have with his sales managers.

Every Business Is Under Siege

Think back to the 1970s when Steve Jobs launched Apple Computer. He enjoyed years of competitive advantage due to his company's technology, graphics, and innovative approach to desktop publishing. Now fast-forward to 2007 and the launch of Apple's iPhone, hailed as one of the greatest consumer innovations in years. In less than six months, competitors copied the iPhone's touch-screen functionality, and its technology was even exceeded in some aspects by Sprint's "Touch" product. This illustrates how every business innovation—even if there is nothing comparable on the market—can lose its competitive advantage within a very short period of time.

In his international bestseller *The World Is Flat: A Brief History of the Twenty-First Century* (Picador, 2007), Pulitzer Prize–winning journalist Thomas Friedman echoes this message: "No matter what your profession . . . you better be good at the touchy-feely stuff because anything that can be 'digitized' can be outsourced to either the smartest or cheapest producer or both. Everyone has to focus on their value add." Friedman goes on to explain that the "touchy-feely stuff" is what delivers real value and business results.

Take a minute to reflect on Friedman's point and then think about your own business and your competition. While your product or service surely stands out to you as being distinctive, it probably does not stand out as such to the potential clients who are assessing your capabilities. The lines of distinction between you and your competitors are much blurrier to them. In fact, many buyers hope that one vendor emerges from the rest so that, in essence, they don't have to flip a coin based on price.

How can you separate yourself from the pack when, in reality, as Jerry puts it, "We all make boxes"? How can you convince prospects today to choose you from among all of the other vendors and service providers vying for their business?

The "Evolving Sales Process"

The speed of the commoditization of business offerings across all industries has resulted in an evolution in the selling process. Selling has by necessity evolved from a show-and-tell *justification* focused on features and functions to a service-oriented *conversation* requiring the client-facing professional to have good listening skills to an approach that results in a solutions-oriented *collaboration* between the buyer and seller. Figure 2.2 illustrates the shifting focus in the sales process since the 1970s.

Many client-facing professionals are naturally more comfortable with the simpler show-and-tell approach. It's based on product knowledge, a general understanding of the value of specific features and functions to a typical client, and a line of reasoning that creates a justification for the sale. All of this is essential to any client-facing professional, of course, but it's not nearly enough today.

Today's competitive climate requires a step change from this comfort zone to the solutions-oriented approach, with its three

Figure 2.2: The Evolving Sales Process from the 1970s to the Present

relationally centered goals. First, the relational approach truly focuses on understanding and knowing the people you're work-

> Begin with the principle of worthy intent and you will inevitably create relational capital — putting you head and shoulders above those who just keep on trying to close the next deal.

ing with and putting their best interests at the forefront so that they are comfortable collaborating around business issues with you. Second, it requires tailoring your responses to the prospective client's real needs. Third, it leads the client-facing professional and potential client to create solutions together that uniquely address these needs. This step change is where the key to your distinctiveness resides — it's the only way to distinguish yourself and your business from all of the other "box makers" out there. When you begin with the principle of worthy intent — that is, to build trust and respect with each client or prospect by putting their needs first — you will inevitably create relational capital which, in turn, will put you head and shoulders above those who just keep on trying to close the next deal.

Relational "Superiority Complex"

In tandem with their tendency to *undervalue* the need to think strategically about their business relationships, 78 percent of business professionals *overestimate* the quality and strength of those relationships. Unfortunately, these executives and salespeople alike usually find this out when it is too late, namely, when a competitor is walking off with a client and friend!

Again, it seems that the avalanche of business technologies over the past twenty years is partly to blame for this overestimation of a corporation's bond with its clients and customers. As much as cell phones and BlackBerry-type devices can help us stay connected, they often serve as an additional barrier to real, in-person communication. Individuals that we thought of as business partners are now coldly referred to as "accounts" or, worse, "revenue streams." Remember that Max helped me realize that if we lose sight of the *real person* on the other end of a call or e-mail, then we miss the opportunity to enrich our business endeavors and our lives with the growth and learning that comes from true interaction with others.

This brings to mind a commercial from the 1980s in which a company president hands out airline tickets to his employees in an effort to get them to reconnect with their clients face-to-face. He explains that business has been declining due to their inability to maintain, let alone advance, their important business relationships. He yearns for the time when business was built on real relationships — even friendships — not on impersonal communication via phone, answering machine, and fax (this was before the advent of cell phones and the Internet). Then, as the president leaves the meeting, an employee asks, "Ben, where are you going?" The president responds, "Out to visit that old friend who just fired us!" The not-subtle-in-the-least message was that his client-facing professionals had lost touch with their clients and needed to reconnect at a relational level to turn around the negative impact on their business.

That Annual Sinking Feeling

Let's say you just left your annual sales kick-off meeting. Like the year before, you've invested hours in learning about new products, new market messaging techniques, and new sales processes and technologies. And, just like the year before, you have that sinking feeling that somehow your life may never change. For two of the surest things you and other client-facing professionals can count on each year are that quotas will increase and that compensation plans will be harder to achieve.

Every opportunity you pursue to overcome these annual challenges involves the need to cultivate and advance a business relationship. You've probably invested very little planning in this area, yet you know these relationships are ultimately the secret to your success. However, since you don't have an accurate or realistic sense of the strengths of your relationships, you don't take a very proactive approach to improving them.

How will you get rid of this annual "man the lifeboats" sinking feeling and gain control over your business relationships? How do you begin to advance from your comfort zone relationships to explore challenging relational opportunities? How do you audit the value of the relationships you have? How do you motivate yourself to aspire to becoming relationally focused?

Goals Are Just Dreams
Until You Write Them Down

The good news is that you don't have to wait for your organization to come up with a plan or process to help you achieve better results by advancing your business relationships. In fact, as I promised at the beginning of this book, you can begin immediately!

To start to improve your most important business relationships, you first need to identify them. Take a few minutes to think about the actual existing relationships that make up your constituent profile. Place yourself at the middle and imagine being surrounded by the groups of people you have relationships with (as shown in figure 2.3).

Now reflect on your objectives for the next twelve months and write down on a piece of paper the names of the five most

Figure 2.3: Constituent Profile

important business relationships that you need to advance to achieve those objectives. (I like to refer to these as your "Fab 5.")

My firm has had great success with clients when we suggest that they initially focus on only five relationships. The main reasons for using that number are the following:

- It creates a sense of priority among the many relationships that client-facing professionals have.
- It is manageable, allowing for follow-up and measurement of advancement or slippage on the Relational Ladder (which I discuss in much more detail in chapter 4).

- It provides the opportunity for diversity in learning and advancement. For example, one brand-new relationship, two or three in process, and possibly one or two at the highest level.

My experience with clients indicates that this apparently simple step actually requires deeper thinking than they anticipated. The reason why is based in the research I shared earlier about how few corporations require their client-facing professionals to connect quota achievement to the advancement of key business relationships. However challenging this step might be, it is worth undertaking because it accomplishes two very important steps on the way to creating relational capital and improving performance:

1. It specifically identifies a Fab 5 business relationship by name, not by the organization where that person works or by the contact through whom you met that person.
2. It attaches each relationship to a performance objective.

As we go forward, you will have the opportunity to actualize what you learn in this step through the creation of your own Action Plan. Your Action Plan will contain the strategies to help you advance your Fab 5 and to take your business endeavors to a new level of success.

Identifying these relationships is the vital first step you must take in shifting how you perceive your role in any business relationship. Instead of just wishing that better business contacts would magically appear in your professional life, you will take the business contacts you've already established to more productive and rewarding levels. The initial step of pinpointing your Fab 5 will lead you toward participating with an actual person rather than with a digital line in a CRM system. And once you are dealing with a real person, you can practice your worthy intentions by learning more about that individual's Relational GPS—their goals, passions, and struggles—which every businessperson has. When you understand your clients' Relational GPS, you'll know which relationships are working and which ones need work, as well as exactly how to go about it. You'll feel like you are no longer leaving business relationships—the most important aspect of your business performance—to chance.

> Great relationships have many intangible rewards, but when the achievement of your life goals is at stake, they also translate to rewards of the more ordinary, tangible sort—the kind that pay the mortgage and send the kids to college.

 ## RELATIONAL INSIGHTS

☑ Relational capital is the prevailing distinguishing element in business today.

☑ Companies that focus on developing relational capital create relational attributes with clients that are difficult for competitors to match.

☑ The distinctive value of your relational capital transcends the immediate transaction and becomes the fingerprint you leave behind as you advance your business relationships toward generating superior performance.

☑ No matter how much you refine your business relationship with a client, additional steps can always be taken to further develop and strengthen that relationship.

☑ The first step to creating relational capital is to identify the five most important business relationships (your Fab 5) that you need to advance in order to achieve your quotas and objectives.

Chapter 3

Essential Qualities:
Credibility, Integrity, and Authenticity

Today is your day; your mountain is waiting, so get on your way.
—Dr. Seuss

For years I struggled to define in business terms Max's abstract wisdom for developing outstanding business relationships. During this process, I learned some interesting facts:

- Such intangible assets as intellectual property, brands, corporate reputation, employees, acquired goodwill, and customer relationships contribute more than half the market value of Fortune 500 companies today.

- These intangible assets are also critical sources of income, referrals, repeat business, financial growth, and competitive distinction.

- In fact, intangible assets comprised of customer, employee, and supplier relationships are so important and valuable that some investors will happily pay a premium to own shares of these companies. This *organizational* relational capital enhances the value of the corporation, making it attractive as a long-term, strategic investment with a higher valuation versus a pure financial investment, which will likely not perform as well.

You can apply this same perception of value when calculating and growing your personal net worth in life and business. Your intangible assets include your knowledge and skills, educational background, reputation, and personal and professional relationships. Your intangible assets create lasting value, such as

- Providing access to business and career opportunities that generate income
- Attracting people and business opportunities to you
- Generating referrals and repeat business
- Creating a network of people that can offer help and resources
- Allowing you to help others
- Making your life and career more enjoyable

These intangible assets can be viewed as aspects of your *relational capital*, which you'll recall from chapter 1, is the distinct value created by people in a business relationship.

Your ability to advance business relationships by creating relational capital with your clients is the most impactful way for you to distinguish yourself in your client interactions. I mentioned the principle of worthy intent earlier as the foundational, or "going in," approach to every business relationship. In the next paragraph I explore the three essential qualities that are at work as you create relational capital in every one of your business relationships.

After many trips in Max's taxi, and throughout the course of my workplace experiences, I came to realize that Max's "little extras" translated into three specific qualities (see figure 3.1) that are at work beneath the surface every time you develop a business relationship. Your credibility, integrity, and authenticity constitute the essential foundation upon which you build relational capital in the business world. These qualities impact how you are perceived and valued, and their convergence results in the relational attributes that attach to you in every business relationship.

Credibility, integrity, and authenticity are present in every business relationship to some degree because each of us possesses

Figure 3.1: Essential Qualities of Relational Capital

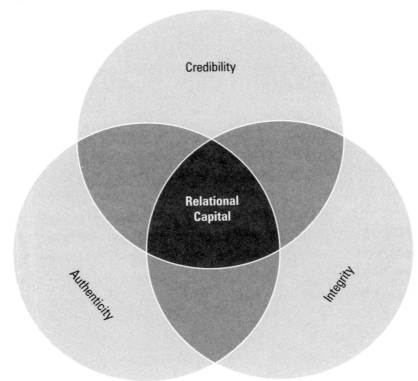

Credibility

Relational
Capital

Authenticity

Integrity

these qualities. In *outstanding* business relationships, however, these qualities form the very basis of the relationship, leading to many competitive advantages and rewards for client-facing professionals. And while each quality is important in its own right, understanding how the three converge is the key to creating relational capital with each business contact.

Many businesspeople perceive these qualities to be very similar; in fact, my clients routinely substitute one for the other during our discussions. Looking closer, however, we can see that there are important fine distinctions among the definitions of each term. And there is a distinct order in how each one manifests itself in a business relationship.

Credibility

Credibility is the quality that makes others believe in you, your words, and your actions. Credibility is the gatekeeper quality. If you don't first establish credibility and competence with your prospect or client, you will struggle to create anything more than a transactional relationship with that individual. Everything about Max, for example, reinforced his credibility: his demeanor, enthusiasm, knowledge, ability to ask questions, and even the way he maintained his taxi reflected his worthy intent to keep my best interests in the forefront of our business relationship. I believed that he was committed to my travel needs, that he was capable and competent to deliver on that commitment, and most important, that he cared about me as a person by making my experience as memorable as possible.

As client-facing professionals, we all want our clients to trust us. Once they do, we can start doing things for them in order to move the process along. However, until we are deemed credible and competent, why would clients trust us with the three elements of their Relational GPS?

Goals — personal long- and short-term business objectives

Passions — business and personal causes and activities they care deeply about

Struggles — obstacles or commitments that are holding them back

Let's look at Relational GPS in a little more depth before we move to the discussion about integrity.

Relational GPS

Driving a car equipped with a GPS (that is, a Global Positioning System) has become a way of life for us as we travel, taking much of the guesswork out of following directions that our parents' generation struggled with. Global positioning systems rely on satellites that orbit the Earth at more than seven thousand miles per hour, synchronizing coordinates and time and then sending signals to the GPS device in your car. It amazes me how accurate these directions are even in construction zones. They are the new road map to our travel success.

Correspondingly, the major part of the road map to our success in developing outstanding business relationships is to understand the Relational GPS of each of our clients. If your clients believe that you can help them deal with their goals, passions, and struggles on both a professional and a personal level, you can advance through the sales cycle much more meaningfully and successfully. The challenge, of course, is that clients — who are people, after all — are generally not inclined to share their goals, passions, and struggles with anyone they do not deem as credible or competent.

The key then (using that road map) is to navigate through the process of launching your relationship and starting to work together. But until clients begin to share their goals, passions, and struggles with you, the business relationship is parked in neutral, which is really only good for going through a car wash.

How do you get in gear and move forward? Let's go back to Max, who was able to turn the act of asking questions into client-identified attributes about him, like listening and remembering, sharing relevant information, and keeping commitments. After his riders began attaching these attributes to him, they shared more and more about their needs, and his business flourished.

> Continue to observe and learn more about each client's Relational GPS because individuals shift their interests and priorities over time.

Only after our clients deem us credible will they begin to ask us to do things for them that align with their goals, passions, and struggles. Keep in mind that you want to continue to observe and learn more about each client's Relational GPS because it is a dynamic process; individuals shift their interests and priorities over time. And as they share more of their Relational GPS with us, we are able to move to the second essential quality of relational capital—integrity.

Integrity

Integrity is, quite simply, being trustworthy in our actions and character. It is doing the right thing when no one is watching, like leaving our business card on the windshield of a car we just bumped in the parking lot. It is saying what we are going to do and then doing it. Integrity is the quality of having honest and truthful motivations for our actions. This translates directly into applying the principle of worthy intent in all of our interactions in the business world.

Everyone wants to believe they can be trusted and can trust others in life and business. Many clients gauge our integrity by the way we make our commitments and deliver on them. After we have established that we are credible, our clients will begin to ask us to make commitments to them in the form of contracting for goods, services, and solutions. When we deliver what we promised, we display our integrity and reinforce the client's trust. In doing so, this opportunity further advances the business relationship and increases the distinctive value of our relational capital.

Max's integrity was evident from the start of our friendship. Fairness, honesty, and ethics were fundamental values to him, evident in how he treated his clients and lived up to his commitments. Remember how he sadly turned away my business because he was already booked for three weeks? He could have easily double booked to ensure a fare for that time and then cancelled later. However, the worthy intent reflected in his integrity would not allow him to inconvenience me or other riders.

Integrity is also about expectations, making sure we set them appropriately and then consistently delivering on them. The old phrase about commitments, "under promise and over deliver," actually contradicts the worthy intent that we should strive to bring into our business relationships.

Authenticity

I shared how our private integrity keeps us honest in our social interactions and that we expect the same in our business relationships. *Authenticity* is about being honest with ourselves and our clients regarding who we are and what we know; it is the quality of being genuine. I believe that authenticity is sometimes the hardest of the three essential qualities of relational capital to demonstrate, and it requires the highest degree of bravery on our part. Why? Because at times in business we can get caught up in our image and how we look in front of clients, especially when we do not have all of the answers.

Max helped me understand that the three most powerful words in business are "I don't know." This simple admission that you don't have all of the answers is refreshingly honest in today's economy. When you have developed an outstanding business relationship, by openly sharing your own struggles and other aspects of your Relational GPS you will open the door for additional opportunities to work even more closely with your clients. In many cases, this can lead to even better solutions.

"Re-appreciating" Max

Max's approach to building outstanding business relationships was founded upon these three essential qualities. He was consistently and continually credible, full of integrity, and authentic. I mentioned earlier that we all have and can exhibit these qualities just as Max did, along with the principle of worthy intent, and I hope you will consider re-appreciating their importance — discovering their apparent value in terms of creating relational capital with every business contact you make.

Max knew that until you are credible, your clients will not be interested in trusting you or exploring how you can help them. But establishing credibility can help you work toward displaying your integrity. That is, as your clients learn to trust you, they begin to share their goals, passions, and struggles, and they ask you to deliver on various commitments. Finally, after you've delivered on those commitments, authenticity comes into play. During this stage your client welcomes your help, even when it is unsolicited or when you have been honest about not having all of the answers.

When you make worthy intent your going-in principle in your business relationships, then credibility, integrity, and authenticity — the three essential qualities for creating relational capital — will be more easily and readily expressed, and you will be well on your way to advancing every business relationship.

Relational Blockers

We all understand both the importance of these three essential qualities in creating relational capital and the value that personal relationships have for our business. But we also need to understand that certain "relational blockers" exist that get in the way of developing outstanding business relationships. Relational blockers are dynamics that prevent us from demonstrating the qualities of credibility, integrity, and authenticity as we advance our relationships with clients and customers. There are six main relational blockers to be aware of, each of which is described in the following paragraphs.

Blocker #1: Feature and Function Obsession

At times we remain in our comfort zones by focusing on the "hard skills" side of our products and service offerings. It feels easier to sell a product or service on the basis of its technical features and functions because we have studied and learned many things about these aspects. Guess what? We also happen to sound a lot like our competitors when we approach clients in this manner.

When you focus on the features and functions of your product, you are not distinguishing yourself in today's commoditized business environment. Feature and functional information is factual information that a prospective client can easily find on a website. To be sure, knowing this information will help your clients understand how your product works, but this knowledge won't necessarily clarify how your product can help them meet their goals—and focusing on it will not add value to your relationship. You don't want to be thought of as a "talking billboard" but rather as someone who thoughtfully seeks to understand each individual client's goals, passions, and struggles.

Blocker #2: Failure to Recognize Your Perpetual Audition

Whether we think about it or not, the quality of the relationships we create is being evaluated constantly by those we are working with. While you may think you are introducing a client to how your offering can help her with a goal or struggle, she may in fact be thinking about whether or not she likes or respects you as a person. She may be asking herself questions like these: Do I believe what this person is saying? Is this someone I can trust and respect? Do we have good working chemistry? Do I really want to do business with him? How will he work with my team?

Forgetting or not realizing that the spotlight is always on us when we are working with our clients becomes a relational blocker because we end up taking our time together for granted. Often we end up "winging it": we go to meetings unprepared and then fail to listen to our client or address her concerns.

Blocker #3: BlackBerry Addiction Disorder

To me, one of the greatest obstacles to better business relationships is our love affair with technology. I call this fixation BlackBerry Addiction Disorder, or BAD for short. Maybe you or someone you know suffers from this condition. A good indication is the manifestation of any of the following symptoms:

- Decrease in manners
- Shorter attention span

- Inability to communicate face-to-face
- Constant ring tone in your ears
- E-mailing a coworker in the office right next to you
- Leaving your BlackBerry on during a client meeting
- Decline in personal and business relationships

I have nothing against BlackBerrys, or any other such devices for that matter. I use one myself. But I think if we're honest with ourselves, we have to admit that we're so enamored of today's instantaneous electronic communications that the technologies have started to take the place of true person-to-person relationships.

For instance, stand outside a hotel conference room after a business meeting breaks and observe the number of participants who try to get to know each other. Usually only a handful of people congregate, while the rest rush off to make calls or send text messages.

> If our clients do not believe that we are engaged 100 percent with them in the moment, we face a relational blocker to advancing our business relationship.

Sometimes we forget how important it is to be in the present — and present! If our clients do not believe that we are engaged 100 percent with them in the moment, a relational blocker to advancing our business relationship will arise.

Blocker #4: Busyness

We think that if we're not in motion all of the time we aren't really getting anything done. So we spend a lot of time making ourselves busy or generating *busyness* for ourselves through texting and emptying our inboxes just so we can check things off our lists.

But what have we really accomplished? Max called this "filling your day with activity," and it can cause you to take your eye off the ball. Busyness became a blocker for me early in my career as I sometimes found myself putting the submission of an expense report ahead of a follow-up call with a client.

Don't get me wrong; I know that I needed to accomplish both tasks to be effective. But the client call certainly should have come first. The problem can occur—and this is why busyness is a blocker—when we perceive the client calls to be more challenging to handle than the expense report submission. Calling the client back means recalling facts from previous discussions, having answers to questions the client asked you to follow up on, and being prepared to possibly hear that the client has decided to work with someone else. Preparing an expense report, on the other hand, seems much easier and less risky to do—until we see our commission check, that is.

Blocker #5: Instant Gratification Is Not Fast Enough

Because we are so accustomed to using our BlackBerrys and iPhones to provide us with instant information, we now demand and expect instant gratification in all of our business interactions. This blocker creates a sense of urgency in our client interactions and can actually negate our efforts to advance the relationship. In other words, clients could feel rushed into making a decision about your product or service or, worse, make a decision based solely on information unrelated to their Relational GPS. As if that weren't bad enough, this sense of urgency also neutralizes the three essential qualities we discussed earlier that should always be distinguishing you among the competition.

This reminds me of a conversation I had with a client of mine named Tracy, a partner in a large public accounting firm. She shared that she was struggling with why her audit team could not find additional opportunities for consulting services with one of their existing clients. After exploring several possible explanations, we realized that nine out of ten of her team's inquiries to clients were sent electronically, yet most clients were not inclined to share their most pressing needs via e-mail. Tracy implemented a new plan immediately: each of her audit team managers would schedule a weekly face-to-face discussion with a given client, to whom they would send — via e-mail — a list of inquiries in advance to best pave the way for the discussion. Using this simple approach, Tracy and her team were able to uncover more of the client's goals, passions, and struggles, which resulted in a 22 percent increase in her practice's revenue the following year.

The key takeaway here is that electronic technology is a tool; when used effectively, it will complement the advancement of a business relationship, not serve as a shortcut to client opportunities.

Blocker #6: Quality Versus Quantity of Relationships

Never before have we been presented with so many business connection opportunities as there are today. Just think of the many electronic social networks available through the Internet, such as Facebook and LinkedIn. Never before in the history of the human race have we felt so connected to each other, globally and locally. Ironically, however, we face being disconnected from one another if we confuse having hundreds of contacts on LinkedIn with having real business relationships. These digital — really "ethereal" — relationships are just lines on a computer screen until we invest the time and effort necessary to explore and learn about a client's Relational GPS.

When I point out to my clients that they are merely fostering these digital relationships, I usually hear: "Well, shouldn't I keep accepting the networking invitations? Otherwise, won't I miss out on valuable opportunities?" The fact is that while technology has allowed us to become deeply immersed in the number of network connections we have achieved, the actual resulting business relationships have never been shallower.

The other frequent comment I hear is, "What am I supposed to do on this networking site, just keep responding to the automatic postings?" This is where the tool can overpower the user and distract him from real and valuable opportunities to meet contacts and begin building relational capital.

If we allow the pace of technology and communications, along with the ongoing commoditization of business offerings, to take our eye off the ball, we are leaving the real business value that will be attained from creating relational capital on the table. Having a bunch of names in your database without any advancement toward objectives and business development holds limited value when compared with the performance you will get from actively developing and strengthening relationships with your Fab 5, among others.

> If we allow the pace of technology to take our eye off the ball, we are leaving the real business value of creating relational capital on the table.

These relational blockers, individually or in combination, can prevent us from experiencing and benefiting from what is going on right in front of us at any given moment, namely, the opportunity to develop an outstanding business relationship.

The next chapter introduces the five steps I've designed to transform contacts into high-performing relationships and describes how the steps merge and align with the principle of worthy intent and your credibility, integrity, and authenticity in a repeatable process. When internalized, this process leads to relational attributes that identify you, distinguish you, and help you develop business relationships that last.

This process-centric approach will take you from the initial stages of a business relationship, where you establish your credibility and common ground with your client, all the way to becoming a Respected Advisor, the point when your expert advice is sought out and valued.

> While I was writing this book, I repeatedly thought of the classic line from *The Godfather*, "Nothing personal, just business!" This might be true in those movie characters' line of work, but I've found through many years of advising clients that in real business, the exact opposite is true: It's not just business, it's personal.

 ## RELATIONAL INSIGHTS

☑ Credibility, integrity, and authenticity are the three essential qualities that converge to form relational capital in every business relationship.

☑ Taken in order, these qualities advance a business relationship. Until we are deemed credible and competent, our clients will not share their Relational GPS with us, and the business relationship will stall.

☑ Clients determine early on your capability to help and work with them based on the way you exhibit these qualities.

☑ Each client has his or her own Relational GPS—that is, both business and personal goals, passions, and struggles. When you understand these deeply, they become your road map to determining what is working, what needs work, and exactly how to go about advancing each relationship.

☑ Relational blockers are dynamics that get in the way of our credibility, integrity, and authenticity in business relationships as we attempt to distinguish ourselves from our competitors.

Chapter 4

Process Makes Perfect

Electricity is really just organized lightning.
—George Carlin

We benefit greatly from models and methodologies because they give us an organized framework for a repeatable process that we can understand and get comfortable with. Processes are also effective because they help us turn activities into routines, repeated behavior we can refine and improve. It's more than logical, therefore, to have a repeatable process that identifies, measures, and proactively improves our most important business relationships.

The Comfort of a Routine

At the most basic level, many of us like the feeling we get from creating a list of the things that we have to do and then checking things off the list. Since humans seek patterns and structure, we feel a sense of accomplishment as we go through lists and processes. Professional athletes provide great examples of the effectiveness of routines. Take baseball players, for instance. They will arrive at the ballpark at a precise time each game day, dress a certain way to warm up, begin warming up to a set number of exercises and repetitions, have batting practice, eat a meal or a snack, and possibly take a shower before donning their uniforms for the game. Each player establishes his own routine and follows it as closely as possible each and every time.

The adherence to this regimen provides the player with a series of accomplishments that ultimately lead him to feel confident that he is prepared to play a superior game. Ted Williams, who many consider the greatest hitter of all time, followed his preparation routine so diligently that he even cleaned his bats every evening so as not to allow any buildup of dirt to develop, which could theoretically add unneeded weight to his bat and impact his swing. He took the field absolutely certain that he had followed his routine and left no stone unturned.

Like professional baseball players, client-facing professionals have routines that are important to our sense of being ready to move through the stages of the day's activities. Most of us don't feel ready to leave the house in the morning until we have completed such tasks as showering and dressing appropriately, having breakfast, packing the kids' lunches, taking care of the pets, and so on. We feel a sense of accomplishment by following through on the routine things we have to get done. It's these kinds of simple check marks that give us the sense of achievement, even confidence, that we are ready for the next set of tasks and activities.

The Relational Ladder

Having a similar sense of accomplishment in how we feel about our most important business relationships can also be very powerful and motivating. With this in mind, I applied all of my experiences with thousands of clients and partner relationships, along with research into client behaviors, to develop the 5 Steps to Transform Contacts into High-Performing Relationships:

1. Establishing Common Ground: launch the relationship
2. Displaying Integrity and Trust: secure the relationship
3. Using Time Purposefully: invest in the relationship
4. Offering Help: share relational equity
5. Asking for Help: realize returns on your investment

Throughout the rest of this book, I explain each of these five steps in a way that will allow you to learn new skills and processes for creating business relationships that last. You will also understand how the other key elements of relational capital—the principle of worthy intent, the essential qualities of credibility, integrity, and authenticity, and a client's Relational GPS—interact within these steps as you create and advance relational capital with your clients.

Visually, the five-step process can be represented by a ladder, which I call, appropriately enough, the Relational Ladder. Even though a ladder is simple by design, it can be used to model increased levels of learning and skill development. You could think of a ladder as a metaphor for advancement, achievement, ascent, and visibility in reaching a goal.

If you think of all your important business relationships as being somewhere on the ladder, you can then better determine which steps you

> The 5 Steps to Transform Contacts into High-Performing Relationships: establish common ground, display integrity and trust, use time purposefully, offer help, and ask for help.

need to take to advance these relationships at any given time. Each rung of the Relational Ladder represents a sequential step that moves you toward your most lasting professional relationships. Naturally, each time you move up a rung, you will feel encouraged that such a goal is attainable. But as in real life, you may sometimes slide down a few steps on the Relational Ladder. Let me describe each part of the Relational Ladder in greater detail to anchor the image in your mind.

The Frame

Each side of the ladder's frame represents your specific skill sets. The right side of the Relational Ladder represents the hard skills, or the "science" of your business approach; the left side represents your soft skills, or the "art" of your business approach (see figure 4.1). We all have developed both types of skills to some extent throughout our careers: beginning with our first part-time jobs as teenagers, we then advanced these skills through higher education and work experience.

Hard Skills: Science   The hard skills a client-facing professional needs in order to be successful include industry knowledge, product knowledge, ability to develop return on investment, technical abilities, sales metric proficiency, and proposal writing skills. Since most competing professionals can master these to a fairly effective degree, the science component in many careers has largely become an aspect of business that everyone is indistinguishably versed in.

Recall from the discussion about relational blockers that I mentioned the Feature and Function Obsession. Many client-facing professionals come to over rely on their product-related hard skills when working with clients, which makes the ladder wobbly. We see this when client-facing professionals lead with an arsenal of

Figure 4.1: Relational Ladder

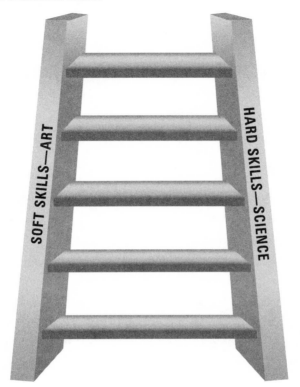

capabilities during their initial discussions with a prospect, failing to gain any sense of what the prospect is trying to accomplish.

In fact, these capabilities are now expected—no, *required*—for client-facing professionals going into most business relationships. Therefore, emphasizing hard skills provides minimal opportunity for these professional men and women to distinguish themselves in the business relationship. However, there is an old saying that brings the value of hard skills into perspective: People do not care how much you know until they know how much you care.

One way you can distinguish yourself with a client is to select and adapt the parts of your technical competency and product knowledge that are most relevant to the specific business situation. Rather than playing back all of your knowledge about every feature and capability of your product and service, learning about specific client goals or passions or struggles helps you align specific elements of your offering to that client's Relational GPS.

> People do not care how much you know until they know how much you care.

Soft Skills: Art On the opposite side of the ladder frame are the soft skills, or the *art* of your business approach. Quite simply, these are your interpersonal skills and behaviors. Some of the soft skills required in business include friendliness, approachability, excellent verbal and written communication skills, listening, managing a network, presentation skills, negotiation, and emotional intelligence. Many executives hire for these skills and assume that the client-facing professional can learn the complementary hard skills required to be successful in the new role. When soft skills are the only competency the professional develops, however, this overemphasized side of the frame causes the ladder to become lopsided and unsteady as well.

We see this with client-facing professionals who believe that investing in continuous social entertaining is the key to unlocking a client's Relational GPS. The challenge with this approach is that in this commoditized world, most competitors have the capability to do the same, which results in this investment of time being no real point of distinction.

The Line Between Strengths and Weaknesses The challenge we face is that we tend to gravitate toward the side of the ladder where we are strongest. Some of us, me included, exercise the soft skills more often, but if someone is best at exhibiting hard skills, he or she will tend to emphasize those strengths. This tendency to *lean* toward where we are most comfortable — thus tipping the Relational Ladder — will eventually make us look to our clients like every other typical client-facing professional.

Picture yourself standing on a ladder. What is the main structural quality of the ladder that you are depending on to keep it from falling to one side or the other? The answer is balance! Developing outstanding business relationships involves carefully balancing science and art, a combination of your hard and soft skills. Neither of these two components should greatly outweigh the other. Think, for example, about the effect of spending all of your time with clients entertaining them instead of talking about business. On the other hand, always talking about technical specifications but never listening to the client or never relaxing enough to get to know him on a more personal level can be just as ineffective.

> Developing outstanding business relationships involves carefully balancing science and art, a combination of your hard and soft skills.

There is an extremely funny scene in the movie *Tommy Boy*. The story is about two traveling salesmen, Tommy (Chris Farley) and Richard (David Spade), who are selling auto parts to small dealers around the Midwest. One prospect expresses interest, so Richard begins a long discourse on the technical superiority of their products. The customer's eyes immediately glaze over. He then turns to Tommy and asks, "Why should I buy from you?"

Tommy, more of a soft-skills guy, begins to role-play, using the prospect's model cars. He demonstrates how his company's brakes will save a family during an accident and that the competitor's brakes will create a major accident. The prospect begins to get interested, but Tommy gets so carried away he accidentally sets the prospect's model car and desk on fire.

While this is a humorous and extreme example of the overuse of hard and soft skills, it can nevertheless help you imagine how your client might perceive you when you heavily rely on one set of skills to the exclusion of the other.

The Rungs

Now that we can visualize our hard and soft skills as the framework for supporting every one of our business relationships, we can think of each of the rungs as one of the steps in the 5 Steps to Transform Contacts into High-Performing Relationships. These steps are the true secrets to success in any business relationship. Applying what you learn from each of these steps will help you identify, measure, and proactively improve how you relate to your Fab 5.

When we place the five steps — establishing common ground, displaying integrity and trust, using time purposefully, offering help, and asking for help — onto the Relational Ladder, you will see how each element has a special role in moving you upward from one step to the next (see figure 4.2):

- Your ability to launch a relationship and move off of the first rung depends on building credibility — becoming believable so your clients will share their Relational GPS with you.

- Your integrity emerges when you deliver on your commitments to your clients time and time again.

- Your ability to reach the top rung of the Relational Ladder depends on creating sufficient relational capital with your clients by reflecting your worthy intent throughout the process to the point where they begin to ask for your point of view — even on issues outside of your business.

Figure 4.2: Relational Ladder: 5 Steps to Transform Contacts into High-Performing Relationships

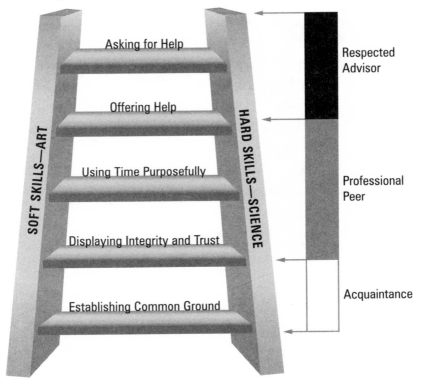

Each of the next five chapters explains in detail a step of the Relational Ladder. You will also see how the principle of worthy intent and the essential qualities of credibility, integrity, and authenticity come into play to help you advance up the ladder to achieve successful business relationships that last.

> Realizing that there is an underlying process that orders the apparent randomness of business relationships is your first step toward gaining—and sustaining—relational fluency.

RELATIONAL INSIGHTS

☑ Advancing your business relationships can be achieved through a focused, repeatable process—your own Relational Ladder.

☑ This Relational Ladder process is reflected in the 5 Steps to Transform Contacts into High-Performing Relationships:

- Establishing Common Ground: launch the relationship

- Displaying Integrity and Trust: secure the relationship

- Using Time Purposefully: invest in the relationship

- Offering Help: share relational equity

- Asking for Help: realize returns on your investment

☑ These five steps are the road map you can use to understand and implement a plan for every business contact.

PART TWO

The 5 Steps to Transform Contacts into High-Performing Relationships

Chapter 5

Establishing Common Ground

You've got to find a way in!
—Rick Reilly, award-winning journalist

It is absolutely crucial to step onto the first rung of the Relational Ladder—namely, establishing common ground—as soon as you meet a new contact. In fact, I dedicated more material and pages to this chapter than any other in this book to ensure that you find a "way in" during the early stages of your business relationships.

At the point of introduction there is a brief window of opportunity when you can start to get to know each other. Say you happen to meet someone—at a meeting, a conference, a social occasion— and you strike up an early acquaintance-type relationship. You begin talking about your business, one thing leads to another, and you reach the point where the person may be willing to discuss doing business with you. The important thing to remember is that although you may like each other at this stage, you don't really *know* each other. The relationship is still more or less at a simple, transactional level. This is naturally where we all begin.

Moving from that level to a committed business relationship begins to happen only when your client shares a goal, passion, or struggle; until that time, your relationship is merely in an Acquaintance dimension. An *acquaintance* is a person you know but are not particularly close to. In business, just as in our personal lives, we seldom share much about ourselves with people we consider to be acquaintances.

Here are some examples of behaviors that acquaintances exhibit in their business relationships:

- Willingness to have a conversation
- Unwillingness to meet after having a few conversations
- Reluctance to offer help or advice related to the business discussion
- Hesitance to share any business goals, passions, and struggles
- Indifference about phone calls or returning e-mails or responding to letters

Before we delve further into the Relational Ladder process, let's take a moment to look into the implications of being a mere business Acquaintance.

Beware the Valley of Acquaintance

All of your business relationships (unless your family owns the company) begin within the Acquaintance dimension. I've found that it's effective to have about 15 percent of your relationships at this level so you can maintain a continuous, actively developing pipeline of new relationships. However, I also recommend that you periodically review your pool of acquaintances and either move each relationship up the Relational Ladder or delete it from this space.

Why? Business contacts whose names languish in the "valley of acquaintance" will not advance their business, your career, or the objectives of either one of you. You don't want to accumulate a large pool of acquaintances who create more *busyness* (remember that old relational blocker from chapter 3?) if they are not developing into something profitable. You should certainly remain friendly and accommodating if you meet, but there is no reason to advance the relationship toward the achievement of your performance objectives.

The onus is on you to invest more at this early stage as the active party who attempts to launch the business relationship and emerge from the valley of acquaintance. There's a flip side to this coin, however. The new people you meet may form a first impression of you that prevents them from letting you take the relationship any further.

> Invest more in the early stage as you attempt to launch the business relationship and emerge from the valley of acquaintance.

There's a famous scene from the comedy classic *Animal House* that makes a relevant point about first impressions. I like to connect the scene to the necessity of advancing beyond the initial Acquaintance dimension in business relationships. The guys at the Delta fraternity house are meeting in their basement to vote on who should be given the honor of joining them. The frat president flashes a photograph of each potential pledge on a screen. Some candidates are met with comments like, "Okay, we need the dues!" But when a picture of a kid named Kent Dorfman is displayed, the room erupts with groans and a hail of beer cans thrown at the screen. The president attempts to regain order and talks in support of Kent but quickly finds that the group's instant negative reactions to the poor applicant—however unfair or unfounded—are already solidified. Surprisingly, as the movie progresses, our friend Kent is able to overcome that initial negative impression, but not without a great deal of effort and personal risk taking.

Think about your initial interactions with past prospects and clients. While their reactions may not have been as animated as in the fraternity scene I just described, your prospects and clients were definitely forming opinions about you based on what they saw and heard. Some experts say that once an impression is formed it's very difficult to change it. That truth gave rise to the old saying "You don't get a second chance to make a first impression." One of my clients has the following title printed beneath the receptionist's name on the front-desk nameplate: Ambassador of First Impressions. This simple but effective phrase immediately communicates a positive message about the way this firm works with its clients.

So, just what is it that people respond to in these first moments of a new business relationship? Certainly what immediately comes to mind are the important "little" things such as punctuality, your clothing, hairstyle, and posture, your handshake and ease in making eye contact, the way you speak, and the attitude and personality you project. If a client has a negative perception of any of these factors, then your business relationship may stumble right from the start. Be sure to pay attention to all of these details so that you lay the solid foundation you need to truly launch a business relationship that will last.

Launching the Relationship

The only goal you should set for your initial meeting is to launch the relationship by establishing common ground while learning about the business opportunity (see figure 5.1). As I mentioned, the onus is on you to make the relational investment up front with a contact, although ultimately the relationship will need to be balanced as you move up the Relational Ladder.

Contacts will certainly respond to the way you *launch* a relationship. You may recall how Max was very skilled at establishing common ground by asking questions in a conversational way

Figure 5.1: Relational Ladder: Establishing Common Ground

SOFT SKILLS—ART

HARD SKILLS—SCIENCE

Establishing Common Ground

Acquaintance

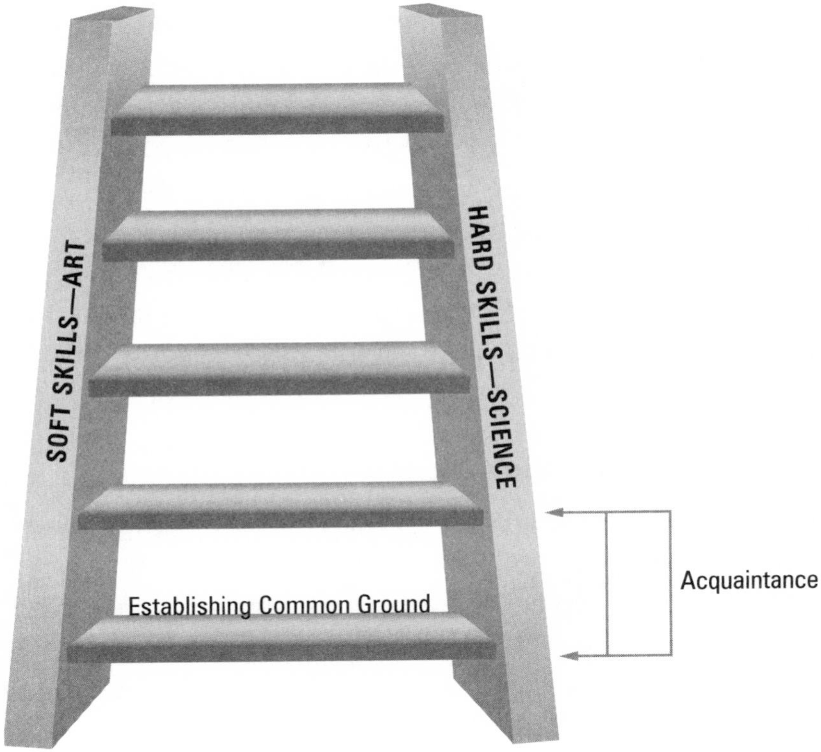

that truly demonstrated his interest, an approach I call "sincere inquiry." Asking questions in this heartfelt manner invites a value-adding conversation—a *collaboration*, even—with the prospect. On the other hand, simply making claims—about your expertise, what your firm can do, etc.—can result in a one-way *presentation* in which it's clear that your main motive is to impress the person or to try to sell her something. This is precisely the way stereotypical client-facing professionals behave and thus fail to distinguish themselves in the first phase of the evolving sales process.

By asking questions, Max learned about my family and our needs, as well as my goals and aspirations. He demonstrated credibility in the way he asked appropriate follow-up questions. In fact, when we discussed my sales endeavors, he was able to ask about my quota, whether I sold on a territory or account basis, and even how much of my sales came from new versus existing customers.

Everything about Max's approach made him credible to me and therefore invited me to share more of myself with him. Reflecting on my experiences with Max, it's clear that he was extremely skillful at establishing common ground, that critical, universal first step in creating relational capital with another person. It was Max, who could find a way to relate to anyone and everyone, who finally showed me how to get to know my very own next-door neighbor.

Mr. DeMarcantonio's Vegetable Garden

Laurie and I once had a neighbor named Mr. DeMarcantonio, who was not very friendly. He kept to himself and spent much of his time tending his vegetable garden, which came up to the edge of our driveway. He was outside in that garden every day, wearing a red baseball cap, digging, weeding, pruning, watering, and generally occupying himself from springtime until fall. I had attempted, albeit somewhat half-heartedly, to hold conversations with him on several occasions, but I never received anything more than a curt hello and a forced smile.

Early one morning I stepped onto my front porch to meet Max for one of my airport rides, and I saw him at the edge of the driveway talking with Mr. DeMarcantonio. Suspicious, I stayed on the porch and watched them. From their laughter and animated gestures, it was obvious they were enjoying each other's company.

After a few minutes, Max noticed me standing there watching them. He said good-bye to Mr. DeMarcantonio, who didn't even glance my way.

"What in the world were you guys talking about?" I asked as we got into the taxi. "I've never been able to get two words out of him!" My frustration was only thinly disguised.

"Tomatoes," Max replied.

"Tomatoes! But how do you even know him?"

"We started talking one morning about our vegetable gardens after he spotted me admiring his. One thing led to another, and on my last trip to pick you up for the airport, I left him some of my tomatoes. Doesn't he have a great garden?"

"Yeah, I guess," I said, intrigued by how Max had broken through Mr. DeMarcantonio's wall. "But, he's never wanted to talk about it with me. I always thought he just wanted to keep to himself."

Max looked at me in the rearview mirror. "Do you really know him to be unapproachable, Ed?"

Max had me on this one. I hadn't invested the time in Mr. DeMarcantonio to be in a position to make that kind of judgment. I guessed Max was suggesting I question my assumptions, especially since I had never made a genuine effort to converse with my neighbor.

"I hear you," I said, "but how do I connect with someone who just doesn't seem interested in connecting?"

"The chances are always pretty good there's common ground somewhere, if you look hard enough to find it."

Come to think of it, Max's entire philosophy for dealing with clients—friends—was finding that common ground. He knew people wanted to feel comfortable, calm, refreshed, and slightly pampered during the ride, and he had created the perfect environment in his meticulously kept taxi to allow this to happen. He knew his customers wanted to talk about themselves, and he was committed to be interested in and knowledgeable about virtually any topic they might bring up. By providing a friendly, relaxing atmosphere, and by making the effort to connect with what was important to his clients, Max had no trouble at all establishing credible common ground, even in a vegetable garden with my surly neighbor.

Getting to Credibility

After I observed how Max established common ground and credibility instinctively, the way most relational rock stars do, I realized that there needed to be an approach for client-facing professionals to use again and again as they begin to distinguish themselves in their business relationships. I thought about the most important areas that surface during an initial client meeting and came up with an acronym, ROC—which stands for **R**apport, **O**bjectives, and **C**redibility—from which you can launch all your business relationships.

Developing the ROC steps also gave me the ammunition for those clients who say, "I'd sure like to interact with people as easily as Max did, but that's just not the type of person I am. How could I possibly learn how to discover common ground with every new potential client I meet?" This next section outlines the three simple ROC steps you can follow—no matter what type of personality you have—to develop an effective approach for finding common ground and creating positive initial meetings in every business relationship you seek to launch and advance.

Using ROC in the Initial-Meeting

The initial-meeting scenario that follows is designed to accomplish three key goals: (1) to help you smoothly establish personal and business common ground, (2) to help you understand when to move between personal and business common ground, and (3) to help you distinguish yourself with your new contacts by demonstrating that you planned the interaction and are not just winging it during your conversation with them. As you'll see, I go into great detail about this approach because you need to emerge from the valley of acquaintance before you can move up to the next step of the Relational Ladder.

To illustrate how to put this into practice, imagine that you are about to meet with a new prospect named Joan. You were introduced to one another at a business convention. Since then you spent some time researching her company's situation and you are confident your company could offer her viable business solutions. You are ready to launch the relationship and find common ground on the way to a lasting business relationship.

ACTION POINT

In preparing for your next initial meeting, learn as much as possible about your potential client by researching the contact's education and professional profile, seeking perspective from people in your network who may know the contact, and scanning the contact's company website and other sources.

ROC Step One: Building Rapport When I find myself in a scenario such as this one, I like to begin with the following statement:

Joan, I appreciate this opportunity to meet with you.

Notice that I am not *thanking* my contact for her time. Every businessperson she meets is likely to begin with "Thank you for your time." Beginning with *thank you* does not distinguish you from the other client-facing professionals she meets, and it implies to Joan from the outset that you feel her time is more valuable than your own. And that, we all know, is not a good start if you are trying to advance the relationship in a balanced way. Plus, the word *appreciate* is just a nice word to use to distinguish you from the rest.

After my brief introductory remark, I pause to allow Joan to signal where she wants to take the meeting. Too often, client-facing professionals try to build rapport in what I believe is an artificial and very risky way. They start by looking around the prospect's office and picking out a picture or some other item—commenting on what a beautiful family Joan has or the diploma from Harvard or the marlin she has mounted on the wall.

In *Creating Relational Capital* (2007), John Holland and I identified the problem with this "too intimate–too soon" approach: What if Joan is having a problem in her family at that particular moment? Do you think she wants to discuss it with you or even to be reminded about it by you, a total stranger, or an acquaintance at best? What if she doesn't feel like talking about her college days? Why take that chance? Rather, eliminate such risks by allowing her to set the tone.

If Joan brings up the weather or asks how helpful her directions were or how your weekend was, then by all means build some rapport by moving into *personal* common ground by answering the question and then asking her a follow-up. Think of a range of neutral topics ahead of time that you might want to ask, depending on where the contact takes the conversation. Examples might be, "How long have you been with the company?" or "Have you always lived in the area?"

The point is *you* are not going to go into the meeting and dictate where the discussion is headed. In our illustration, this is Joan's meeting, and you can allow her to lead the way by giving her the opportunity to make *the first common ground decision.*

If, on the other hand, Joan opens with, "What do you have?" or "So, what can I do for you?" or if Joan does not respond at all to your opening comment, I advise that you go directly to *business* common ground, which is your meeting objective, or the O in ROC.

ROC Step Two: Sharing the Meeting <u>O</u>bjectives   The stage is set for your first discussion with Joan. After an appropriate period of building rapport with one another, or if Joan signals to get right down to business, you will make a transition to the second step of the ROC approach, sharing the meeting objectives. A natural way to do this is to say something like,

> Joan, what I'd like to do today, if you agree, is to take a few minutes to briefly introduce myself and my firm, and then to *learn* more about your new manufacturing process.

Words such as *learn* and *discuss* are great to use at this stage. They are friendly, exploratory, and inclusive, as well as not being aggressive, intimidating, or threatening.

I recommend as part of your meeting preparation that you write out three or four ideas for the kinds of things you want to learn about or discuss in your meeting. Keep these firmly in mind from the start and try to cover as many as possible during the time you are with each prospective client.

The natural follow-up to stating what you would like to learn about and discuss with Joan is to get a clear understanding of how you two will proceed with the meeting. Here's how I would embellish my earlier statement about sharing the meeting objectives:

> Joan, what I'd like to do today, if you agree, is to take a few minutes to briefly introduce myself and the Relational Capital Group. I'm equally interested in *learning* more about your manufacturing process and *discussing* your implementation plan so that by the end of our meeting we can decide together how best to proceed.

(Note: After you share the meeting objectives with your client, remember to confirm that she is aligned with this approach before proceeding.)

If you can get to the point of agreeing about the objective of the meeting right on the spot, you've already achieved a number of advantages. You have

- allowed Joan to set the tone for the meeting;
- shown that you didn't come to waste her time with chitchat;
- revealed that you came to the meeting prepared but that you are flexible and open-minded as to how the conversation could proceed;
- conveyed that you're asking for her input and agreement on how you will move ahead together;
- communicated that there will be an end point for the meeting;
- started creating credibility for yourself; and
- demonstrated, most important of all, your respect for Joan, her time, and her priorities.

Each item in this list results from just a few statements and behavioral approaches. And as you might have guessed by now, Max would call these "the little extras" in turning fares into friends.

ROC Step Three: Developing Credibility At this point in the meeting you need to begin building on the credibility you've just demonstrated so that your contact can continue to assess whether you are a person she would like to consider meeting again and eventually share some of her business goals, passions, and struggles with. Remember, your goal for this meeting is to launch the relationship, that is, to begin to establish some common ground and distinguish yourself from any of your competitors that Joan is meeting — while learning about the opportunity.

The following questions represent what you can say as the appropriate next step after you and the prospective client have agreed on the meeting objectives. Their content, along with the way you ask them, will go a long way toward establishing your credibility and competence.

- "Joan, I mentioned earlier that I would like to learn more about the new manufacturing process your company is planning. How do you see this process impacting the company's overall performance, and how will it help you with your responsibilities?"
- "What is your company trying to accomplish strategically with this new manufacturing process?"
- "How has the current business environment impacted the planning for this project?"
- "How is the implementation proceeding?"

The idea in this step is to open with a question that conveys your sincerity and competence regarding the topic you're discussing and then to follow up with other questions that reinforce that credibility. Underscore both your sincerity and your competence by posing confirming questions to which your client answers with a simple yes or no.

ACTION POINT

Prepare for your next initial client meeting by developing relevant questions about topics that you plan to "learn about" during the interaction.

Equally important in ROC Step 3 is to share your company's value statement with the potential client. Here are some examples of corporate value statements:

- We help clients reduce their business risks by partnering with them on the right type and degree of services.
- We help clients improve their employee benefits by collaborating with them about available options.
- We help clients increase their performance by developing key business relationships.

I have found that when several client-facing professionals from the same firm participate in a workshop, varied responses emerge during this value statement exercise. The challenge for management, therefore, is first to understand that this is problematic and second to consider developing a common value statement for everyone.

ACTION POINT

Develop a value statement—a short, consistent summary of how your company helps clients—that you can begin to use consistently during every initial meeting.

After you have shared your value statement with your prospective client, briefly explain more about your firm. Include at this stage in the conversation points such as when your company was founded, who some of your clients are, what types of projects you've worked on, etc.

You will have noticed, then, that offering your firm's value statement is a natural follow-up to the credibility-enhancing questions you asked in the opening moments of this developing credibility step.

ROC—building Rapport, sharing the meeting Objectives, and developing Credibility—is an effective and rock-solid (the pun is fully intended) approach for establishing personal and business common ground, and credibly launching the relationship. Mastering the three easy, repeatable steps I just described (and as shown in figure 5.2) will provide you with numerous benefits, among them that you

- internalize the idea of building rapport by expressing appreciation for the opportunity to meet and by letting the client set the initial tone for the meeting;
- are prepared to share what you want to learn about or discuss;
- can explain how your firm helps its clients;
- are reminded of the challenges and topics you wanted to learn about and discuss;
- create a favorable impression in your new contact's mind; and
- begin to establish credibility in your new business relationship, to which you'll add integrity and authenticity later on.

Figure 5.2: Using ROC in the Initial Meeting

Initial-Meeting Scenario

1. Building Rapport

"Joan, I appreciate this opportunity to meet with you."
Pause for Joan to set the tone.
If appropriate, establish personal common ground: "How long have you been with the company?"

2. Sharing the Meeting Objectives

"Joan, what I'd like to do today, if you agree, is to take a few minutes to briefly introduce myself and my firm, and then to learn more about your new manufacturing process."

3. Developing Credibilty

Ask questions that convey your sincerity and competence.
Share your company's value statement, such as "We help clients increase their performance by developing key business relationships."

ACTION POINT

Reflect on an initial meeting that did not go very well and determine whether you were misaligned with your client's desire to share business or personal common ground.

Let me add one more observation here about the significance of ROC. We live in the midst of an explosion of communication technologies and innovations, which often lead to diverse cross-cultural and cross-generational relationships. As I was completing this book in a local coffeehouse, I overheard three college students talking about their Facebook pages. I had been struggling with how to weave the new ways people network socially into the fabric of creating relational capital, which is entrenched with meeting

in person or at least face-to-face over a videoconference. So I introduced myself and shared my dilemma.

One student commented: "Eventually, you meet people in real life and then you request them to join. I would never 'friend' someone on Facebook prior to meeting them." I was at once overjoyed as well as cautious because this was only one data point. However, if you think about this student's comment and apply it logically to business relationships, why would anyone electronically "friend" you in any meaningful way? Why would someone share her Relational GPS without ever meeting you in person or engaging with you through multiple videoconferences? ROC provides an effective and respectful structure for that all-important first business meeting.

Why ROC Matters

As the scenario with Joan proves, ROC is a powerful approach to use when you meet with potential clients for the first time. Remember that you are on the first step of the Relational Ladder at this point; you are just getting to know each other, which means you should be focused solely on the task of establishing common ground — and therefore credibility — with your contact. To that end, the ROC approach provides you with the opportunity to demonstrate your worthy intent and helps you advance beyond being merely in the Acquaintance dimension.

This is so important I am repeating the benefits of using this approach to burn them into your memory. ROC helps you internalize the idea of building rapport by expressing appreciation for the opportunity to meet with a new contact and by letting the client set the initial tone for the meeting. You will also be prepared to share what you want to learn about and discuss with your client in a way that leads to your credibility on the challenges and topics that are shared. You establish credibility by adding value to the other person's day and by engaging in discussions that speak to his or her needs and concerns. Finally, ROC is all about developing initial opportunities to *distinguish* yourself from other client-facing professionals.

ROC YOUR INITIAL MEETINGS!

The three steps of the ROC model (building **R**apport, sharing the meeting **O**bjectives, and establishing **C**redibility) help you become relationally fluent when launching your business relationships by

- thinking the meeting through ahead of time;

- asking genuine, sincere, relevant questions that your contact will be interested in;

- learning to take your time, being flexible, and being ready to go with the flow of conversation; and

- avoiding the urge to offer solutions too early in the relationship.

Many professionals—especially those with a great deal of experience—come to take the initial client meeting for granted. They see themselves as experts in their fields, as being so strong in the hard-skills areas that all they have to do is impress the client with their knowledge and expertise. But in doing so, they completely neglect the fact that first and foremost the client needs to know they care.

In working with large professional service firms, I found that some of the most senior people, the partners and sales executives, were short-circuiting the process of the interview with the prospective client. These senior client-facing professionals believe that they know all the questions and how the contacts will respond, so they take shortcuts during the important early stages of the business relationship. The result is that the prospects believe they'll be treated just like everyone else if they do business with these "experts"; they instantly recognize that "These guys don't care about me or my company."

When I encounter professionals who behave like this, I suggest they take a step back and start at the beginning, namely, to go through the ROC process step-by-step. Your prospective clients do not know or care whether you have been through this routine one time or a hundred times. To them, their time and their Relational GPS are the only things that matter. If they think you are ignoring these key factors, you will look like all the other client-facing professionals they are auditioning—and you'll be readily forgotten.

Following the ROC approach guarantees that you will build credibility degree-by-degree through showing clients not only that you and your organization are qualified to help them but also that you are interested in them on a personal level. By demonstrating that you want to learn about things that are important to the client, you create a person-to-person connection. You ask about the person's own goals and aspirations. You seek to understand his or her business issues and current challenges. And, above all else, you will learn to *resist* the urge to offer solutions.

Resisting the Urge to Offer Solutions

The absolute biggest mistake that client-facing professionals make when an initial meeting is positively moving along is offering ways to help the potential new client. While you are on the first step of the Relational Ladder, the client *does not care* about your solutions. In other words, the client does not want your help—yet!

During your initial meeting, when you are launching the business relationship, the contacts are getting to know you, determining whether they can trust you, and deciding whether they want to work with you. Think of Kent Dorfman from *Animal House* (would anyone have listened to a thing Kent said before getting to know him?), and then ask yourself, "Why, at this point in the process, would a prospective client care about what my company can offer?"

> While you are on the first step of the Relational Ladder, the client *does not care* about your solutions.

Even in situations in which clients say to me, "They were giving me all the classic buying signals!" I recommend that they resist offering a solution and pricing at this initial-meeting stage. Let's pick up my conversation with Joan after I've completed Step 3 of the ROC model. I assure you that you will continue to distinguish yourself most successfully if you respond as in the following example:

Joan: Thanks, Ed, for sharing that info about yourself and your company's capabilities. Can you provide me with a sense of what solutions you would recommend and some pricing information?

Ed: I appreciate the info you've shared with me about the project, Joan. What I'd like to do at this point is to take a step back to reflect on what you shared, discuss your project with my team back at the office, and then get back to you with some suggestions on how we could help you.

This approach conveys to Joan that her situation is very important to you—as it should be—and that a standard, off-the-shelf solution to the situation may not work. Here's where you need to take a deep breath and tell yourself that really great things *will happen* when you resist the urge to offer a solution too soon. Those really great things include, among others, the reality that

- You can get smarter about the company's or her team's needs by stepping back and reflecting on what Joan shared about them.

- You will likely come back with a higher-value concept or solution through collaboration with your manager and colleagues.

- You will come back with "suggestions" that will invite collaboration rather than a proposal or recommendations that lead to decisions Joan may not be ready or able to make.

- You will likely continue to distinguish yourself from the other vendors that Joan is meeting with.

Time and time again, I've found that client-facing professionals will leave value on the table if they respond on the spot to a question such as the one Joan proposed in this situation. By shooting from the hip, you may end up shooting yourself in the foot.

Resisting the natural instinct to offer solutions and answers as your client begins to share his or her Relational GPS is counterintuitive and goes against what most client-facing professionals have learned to do. But why behave like all of your competitors? How will that distinguish you in the early phases of your business relationship?

> By shooting from the hip, you may end up shooting yourself in the foot.

Try to remember that while they are assessing your credibility and competence, your clients really do *not* want your help.

The Handwritten Follow-up Note

I frequently ask my clients how they follow up an initial meeting with a prospective client. I find that in nine cases out of ten, they follow up by sending an e-mail. I previously discussed the importance of looking and behaving differently during your initial meeting so that your contact can distinguish you from your competitors. While it may be more convenient and efficient for you to send an e-mail, you can be certain that your message will get lost amid the fifty or so other e-mails your contact receives that day.

To distinguish yourself from your competitors, I suggest that you send a personalized, handwritten note within a day of your initial meeting. When I ask workshop participants why they believe this could be effective, they usually reply that the handwritten note

- will probably be the only one the client receives that month;
- requires the client to physically connect by manually opening your communication;
- will further pay off your worthy intentions that you care about the interaction;
- demonstrates that you are a good listener, you pay attention to detail, and you are organized—attributes that enhance every business relationship;
- provides a vehicle to confirm follow-up steps; and
- demonstrates that you care about the growth of the relationship and the opportunity.

The most important thing to bear in mind is that you send a personalized letter that refers specifically to the meeting the two of you had. (See figure 5.3 for an example of what to write.) Avoid sending a generic "form letter" response. A form letter will seem cold and mechanical, and it will not convey the idea that you thought the meeting was special.

Here's an example, written on the stationery that I use. Feel free to develop your own stationery using this format, as many of my clients have.

Figure 5.3: Handwritten Follow-up Note

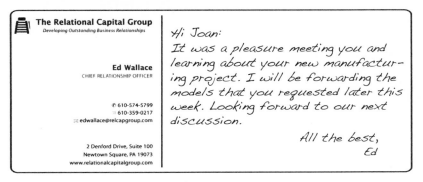

You might think that writing a note is laborious and time-consuming, but as this brief example shows, it's not as labor intensive as you may think. For example, keep a small supply of note stationery (letterhead and envelopes) in your computer bag, along with a book of stamps. As soon as you get into your car after a meeting, take out a sheet of stationery, write out your note, address the envelope, and then mail it on your way to your next call or home. This accomplishes three things concurrently:

- It provides an immediate thank-you and follow-up to the meeting.
- It allows you to write while your thoughts from the meeting are still fresh in your mind.
- It does not get lost on your desk at the office, never to be thought of again.

Keep your notes brief and to the point, but remember to refer to specifics from your launch meeting to make each note as personal as possible. You can always follow up your thank-you note with an e-mail a day or two later, of course, and always remember to send whatever information you promised to send! You want to give every potential client many reasons *not* to forget you.

My favorite handwritten-note story involves a simple service station. For more than thirty years, my partner, Jim Mullen, has been buying his gas from and having all of his auto repairs done by a local, family-owned station in Lafayette Hill, Pennsylvania. They pump your gas and call you promptly to authorize repairs. They will even drive you back to your house and then pick you up after the repairs are completed.

Service is so exceptional, in fact, that after you have repair work done, the owner, Mike, sends a beautiful handwritten note that shows the original service station before it was remodeled and expresses his heartfelt appreciation of your continued patronage.

Mike's service station reminds me of Max and his taxi in that both Mike and Max have commodity businesses, but each one does a lot of the "little extras" to ensure that their attributes are distinguishable to their clients. Do you think that Jim will ever go anyplace else for auto services?

ACTION POINT

Send a handwritten note after each of your next three initial meetings even if the meeting did not conclude with another opportunity.

A Little Extra

A considerable amount of thought and time should be invested in establishing common ground and developing credibility because without these you can't launch the relationship and move out of the valley of acquaintance. Helping clients to believe in you — your personality, your professional standing, your basic competence, your values and ideas—is fundamental to creating relational capital. It's the price of admission to the business relationship. The chances of advancing up the Relational Ladder are significantly increased when you make this investment.

And now you can "ROC" with all of your clients by using this simple, repeatable process for your initial meetings with new contacts. You may remember that my friend Max mentioned the importance of the little extras that allowed him to turn fares into friends. Everything about the ROC process is a "little extra"—the way you go about the meeting, the way you establish credibility through sincere inquiry, and even the way you send a follow-up note. Together the steps in the ROC approach make up the little extras that distinguish you from the rest as you climb the Relational Ladder beyond your initial meetings.

This discussion of the ROC approach reminds me of one particular example from my career that underscores its value, and I'd like to share that with you now.

Dr. Fred

Years ago, when I started my own business providing billing and claims services to physicians, I struggled to leverage every ounce of sales skills I had. At the time, I had no customers, few prospects, and no money. I had been making dozens of sales calls to doctors' offices, leading with my products and services and using typical sales techniques. This resulted in sales figures that wound up right where you might expect them to be—marginal at best.

On one such call I found myself in the basement of a row house in an economically challenged neighborhood. Sitting in the small, wood-paneled waiting room, I noticed several books about walking with the doctor's name printed on the cover of each. He clearly believed in the health benefits of walking, and it was clear that he wasn't very shy about getting that message across to others. I was a runner at the time, so my interest was naturally piqued.

I had read a few pages and become engrossed in a chapter on how much more beneficial walking was compared to running when a nurse called my name and then escorted me to an examining room, where I waited for the doctor.

When the doctor entered, he asked, "What are your symptoms?" without even looking at me.

I cleared my throat and told him that I wasn't a patient, I was there to see him about his accounts receivable.

He took my card, glanced at it, and said, "Mr. Wallace, you have sixty seconds, and you have just used fifteen."

At this point, all of my sales training flew out the window and my instincts kicked in. After what was likely the longest five-second pause of my life, I took a deep breath and replied, "Doctor, I realize that you're very busy, but I can't possibly do justice to explaining my services in the amount of time left to me. Could I ask you a question, though?"

"Shoot," he said.

"In your waiting area, I noticed that you've authored several books on walking. I'm a runner, and I'd love to know why you believe walking is better than running."

The doc's face brightened.

"I'll tell you why walking is better," he said. "Do you ever notice the faces of people who are running?"

"They look contorted."

"Exactly. Now, how do the people walking look to you?" he asked.

I got the point. He not only answered my question, he then went on for thirty minutes to tell me why I should start walking and why he was so passionate about the subject. He also began talking about his latest book. I learned, too, that everyone called him Dr. Fred.

While we were talking, Dr. Fred's office manager tapped on the door three times. The good doctor was on a roll, however, and each time she knocked, he waved her away. Finally, he paused, looked at me, and asked, "What were you here to see me about again?"

I explained that my firm helped doctors improve their cash flow and that I was hoping to learn more about his accounts receivable process. He told me to make an appointment with his office manager, Jane, and then handed me one of his books. "Take this, he said, "and start walking tomorrow!"

During the next few weeks as I worked with Jane, I discovered that Dr. Fred had the largest Blue Cross practice in the entire area. Despite his humble office environment, he saw close to sixty patients per day. My approach with Dr. Fred ultimately led to him becoming one of my largest accounts and—with full credit to Max—*one of my best friends.*

If I had to attribute the sudden turnaround in that first conversation with Dr. Fred to something, I would attribute it to the principle of worthy intent and having watched Max and Mr. DeMarcantonio talk about tomatoes. That day, Max helped me realize that I should always relate to people at a sincere, personal level by making the effort to find the common ground from which to start building a relationship—even when given just one minute to do it!

> Finding common ground is your first opportunity to establish credibility and competence in your business relationships. It's your "way in."

RELATIONAL INSIGHTS

☑ Business relationships do not begin until your clients share their Relational GPS—goals, passions, and struggles.

☑ Your goal for an initial client meeting is to focus on advancing the relationship, which often means securing the second meeting.

☑ Establishing personal and business common ground is the initial and most important step in developing credibility with your client. It begins to move your relationship out of the Acquaintance dimension and up the Relational Ladder.

☑ Helping clients to believe in you—your worthy intent, your personality, your professional standing, your basic competence, your values and ideas—is fundamental to launching the relationship.

☑ ROC is the repeatable process that you can learn to use for every initial client meeting to demonstrate your worthy intent, to begin to establish common ground and credibility, and to distinguish yourself from your competitors.

Chapter 6

Displaying Integrity and Trust

There are no trust-neutral interactions.
—Great Places to Work Institute

Once you've established common ground and credibility with your new client—in other words, you've begun to ROC and roll—you will have recurring opportunities to display your integrity and trust. This allows you to continue to travel out of the Valley of Acquaintance by moving further up the Relational Ladder to become a Professional Peer. At this point you are in a position to display your integrity and build trust because your client is ready to share his Relational GPS in a way that you can commit to and work together on as you advance your business relationship.

Professional Peer

The Professional Peer dimension is the level where you should strive to place and maintain the majority (that is, about 75 percent) of your business relationships. At this level, your business client values you professionally and views you as a peer, with no sense of subservience or hierarchy in the relationship. Whether the client is the buyer of your services or the CEO, each of you strives to work toward the collaborative accomplishment of objectives without any hierarchical dynamics getting in the way.

Just as contacts in the Acquaintance dimension of the relationship displayed certain behaviors, Professional Peers likewise will exhibit early-stage common behaviors that you can observe and respond to in the business relationship. Among these behaviors are the following:

- They begin to share some business goals, passions, and struggles—their Relational GPS—with you.
- They share aspects of their strategy.
- They start to share some confidences.
- They respond in a timely way to your correspondence.

The Professional Peer dimension is where most business relationships need to be. Working at this level ensures that each party is credible and trusts each other with their Relational GPS. Hierarchy in the relationship is minimized as each person works toward mutual benefit.

ACTION POINT

Think of three specific examples of Professional Peer behavior that you or one of your clients has exhibited recently.

Your Client *Contracts* with the Integrity You Display

If your client is comfortable enough with you to begin sharing his goals, passions, and struggles—in his business or as an individual—then a strong element of trust is developing. In other words, he sees you as someone credible and someone in whom he can share confidences. He may, in fact, be providing you with information that reveals a weakness or liability on a personal or business level that he has concerns about. Because you have already established credibility on the first step of the ladder, he

> Integrity is the foundation of trust and the means to securing the relationship.

is now looking for more reasons to trust you, to have confidence in your integrity. He is giving you an invitation to move up to the next step (see figure 6.1), where proving your integrity through actions secures the relationship.

Figure 6.1: Relational Ladder: Displaying Integrity and Trust

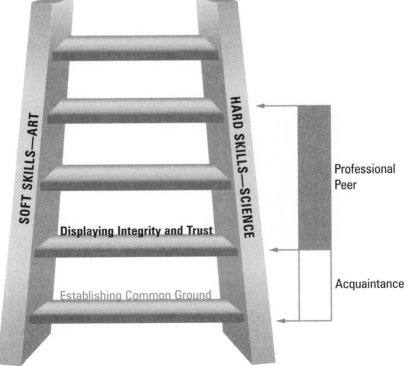

I mentioned earlier that integrity is defined as displaying trust-worthiness in our actions and character; it is saying what we are going to do and then doing it. This is sometimes viewed as a private quality because we do the right thing in many circumstances when no one is watching. There is also a public side to integrity, however, and that is when we make and keep business commitments. Both the public and the private sides are explored in the following pages.

Private Integrity: "No Cutting in Line"

The private side of integrity is that it must be part and parcel of your character. I learned to re-appreciate "private integrity" through one journey in particular with Max.

On one of our morning rides, I asked Max if he ever picked up a random fare at the airport after he dropped me off before he picked up another scheduled friend—in order to *Max*imize his income. "It seems like a waste of time just driving down here with me and not driving back with a fare," I said.

"Well, Ed" (whenever he prefaced his answer in this way, I knew Max was going to deliver some pearl of wisdom), "you're right; I do have an opportunity to do that every time I drop my friends off here." Then his voice kind of trailed off. "I actually did it once when I was first getting started—dropped off a friend and went right around to Arrivals and picked up the next person in line."

"It must have been a profitable trip for you," I said.

"Not really," he replied, sounding more serious than I expected.

"Why not?"

"What time is your flight?" he asked. We had just entered the airport complex. I told him I had another ninety minutes.

"Can you stay with me for a few more minutes, then? I want to show you something."

Max circled around to an outlying lot on the way to the Arrivals section of the airport. "Do you see that parking lot, with all of the yellow taxis lined up?"

"Sure. Man, there are a lot of taxis over there!"

"Yes, and you know what else? Some of them have been there for hours," he sighed.

"Wow," I said, "they need to find a way to avoid that line."

Max paused. He knew I was still not getting it. Then he tried again.

"Ed, most of those guys are immigrants who have no education. They come to this country, somehow find money to lease a taxi, work from dawn to midnight, never see their families, and spend a great deal of their time in that line. The unwritten rule is that if you want an arrival fare, you wait in that line."

"So," I said, "one day, without knowing all of this, you picked up a fare and cut some other guy out of a fare to the suburbs."

"Yes, Ed, and to this day I regret it. I won't do it again."

"Oh, come on, Max, it was only *one fare*," I said, attempting to exonerate him.

"Yes, it was only one fare, but I didn't play by the rules. Who knows, maybe that next driver in line only picked up a short, local fare for all of the time he spent waiting—because I cut in line and took the larger suburban fare. Someday, I hope the airport will regulate the process better. But, whether they ever do or not, I need to do my best to abide by the unwritten rules, the ethics of my profession."

My experience with Max and the taxi line was very compelling. I realized just how private the quality of integrity can be. It's really something to be proud of when our friends say, "She certainly has integrity," but it's even more powerful for us as individuals to live it without any acknowledgment. The airport taxi situation at that time was wide open for abuse, without any accountability, yet Max lived his integrity in the face of no real consequences other than, of course, his own requirement to sleep at night.

We run into private integrity tests every day when we estimate mileage on our expense reports, quote fees to clients in competitive situations, or record the number of hours we bill to a client. Practicing private integrity simply means doing the right thing at all times.

ACTION POINT

Come up with a few examples of times when you exhibited private integrity without anyone else knowing what you had done.

Your Client *Contracts* with the Trust You Build

Just as important as the integrity that you display in business relationships is the trust that you build in those relationships. The Great Places to Work Institute, a research firm that studies the dynamics that make a workplace great for employees, recently shared that there are no trust-neutral interactions. Every occasion in which you have the opportunity to interact — that is, to listen, to provide information, to do a favor, to follow up on fulfilling a promise — represents an opportunity to *build* trust or to *damage* trust, either by not following through or not proving to be true to your word.

Commitments are the promises we make in business. Avoid at all costs making promises during your business discussions that you know you can't keep. Even if a promise is made casually, somewhere along the line you'll be held to your word. Failing to produce what you've promised will atrophy the relationship and close the door on any future opportunities. In sharp contrast, delivering what you've promised will build trust in the relationship and open the door to many future opportunities.

We are all fundamentally honest, and we want to be *consistently* viewed as trustworthy in our interactions with others. This takes a large measure of commitment—the determination to stick with our standards whether it is convenient or not.

ACTION POINT

Think of any recent client promises that you have been slow to keep.

I gave a talk recently at a state university. Walking down a hallway en route to the auditorium, I noticed the following words of wisdom tacked up on a bulletin board. I couldn't find anyone who knew where the paper had come from or who had written the words. After some research I found that most of the passage came from none other than Abraham Lincoln, which somehow didn't surprise me, nor will it surprise you as you read the words.

Commitment
Commitment is what
transforms a promise into reality.
It is the words that speak
boldly of your intentions
And the actions which speak
louder than words.
It is making the time
when there is none
coming through time after time,
year after year after year.
Commitment is the stuff character is made of,
the power to change
the face of things.

It is the daily triumph
of integrity over skepticism.

Keeping Your Commitments

Whenever I read that quotation, I think about my friend Kevin who owns one of the most successful residential painting contracting businesses in the United States. He regularly is invited to be a keynote speaker at industry events, and he has become a noted consultant to his fellow painting contractors. In fact, he and his brother, Brian, have created a second business where they advise and coach a select group of high-performing painting contractors on how to run their businesses.

Well, keeping his commitments happens to be the highest value and secret to Kevin's success. How did keeping commitments help Kevin become so successful?

During his college years, Kevin came to the realization that he wanted to create his own business rather than pursue a corporate track. He wanted a business where he could see the results immediately and also live and share his still-evolving yet altruistic philosophy about how to run a successful business. He did some part-time painting for a local contractor during one summer and then realized that he could do the same on his own. During his senior year he began to drop advertising flyers in mailboxes during his morning jogs. Then on the weekends, he would stop by the houses where he had left the flyers and introduce himself, and he eventually earned some painting jobs. Kevin was very skilled at having initial meetings.

Around the same time, Kevin observed how his parents were a bit unnerved at how long a contractor was taking to install a new bathroom in their home. In fact, it took this particular contractor more than a year to convert a closet into a bathroom, a relatively simple project. The situation was exacerbated because the contractor kept promising various dates for the project's completion and never kept one of them. Kevin's mother was not particularly pleased with this and made sure that her neighbors knew all about it.

As Kevin asks, "Do you think that contractor ever got any more work in our neighborhood?"

This helped Kevin sharpen his view about commitments as he continued to build his business from his dorm room. Kevin approached every potential customer with his parent's experience in mind and emphasized living up to every commitment. For example, Kevin will paint and repaint and repaint a project until his customer is satisfied. He has an unmatched reputation for his commitment to customer satisfaction. His business performance speaks for itself. After thirty years and more than thirty thousand completed painting jobs, not to mention hundreds of repeat customers, Kevin continues to keep his promises at every step along the way.

ACTION POINT

Think about any recent commitments that a colleague or client has made to you. Have they delivered on their commitments?

Tracking Your Commitments

Client-facing professionals must make — and deliver on — commitments regularly in order to move the sales cycle along. Some of these commitments are made to the client and her team while others are made to the internal team that is supporting the sales process. But while making and keeping your commitments are critical, it's equally important to communicate to your clients exactly what you have done for them. You can't do this effectively unless you have tracked your progress on your commitments with hard facts.

Therefore, after you've delivered on your commitments, you'll want to

- Ensure that your client *knows* that you have delivered on your commitments
- Keep the client apprised of next steps and developments
- Update your client after you are sent out on referrals
- Provide factual proof — not hype — to support your commitment

I want to take a moment here to emphasize the importance of the last point on that list — using facts more than hype to communicate exactly what you have done. To make this point, let me share with you a brief story about a brush that I had with greatness.

A few years ago, I had the good fortune to be seated on a flight next to Hall of Fame sportscaster Dick Enberg. While I'm sure that he wouldn't remember our conversation, meeting him was a big deal to me. It brought back a flood of memories, hearing his voice announcing games and his signature exclamation "Oh my!" during every great sporting event — the Olympics, the Super Bowl, the World Series.

But besides his signature line and great voice, what makes Dick Enberg so memorable to me, and the reason why he's had such a positive influence on his profession, is his effective use of factual information to convey his points to the broadcast audience. While the "color analysts" working with him are formulating their *opinions* about the players and teams, Enberg focuses his analysis strictly on the *facts*.

For instance, on one occasion he was covering a professional football game that involved a team whose offense had not been doing well for several weeks. The analysts immediately talked about how awful the offense was and gave their opinions about how the team would do in this game, and why. Enberg, on the other hand, got down to facts: he explained that over the last four games the team had not scored even one time during the first quarter; he cited that they had advanced the football fewer than fifty yards during each quarter. He paused and didn't offer any opinions. The facts were all that he needed to make his point; no embellishment was required.

The key lesson in this is that when you're working to advance a business relationship and you want to communicate what you've done (that is, what you've accomplished on their behalf by following through on your commitments), you'll make your strongest case by giving the client just the facts that support your claim. If the facts are clear and attention getting — you've researched some important information and have a printed report to share with them; you've contacted an expert in a position to help them with a technical problem, etc. — you will not need to resort to a smoke screen of words, trying to give an impression of being helpful. Strong facts will best support your claims and help you fulfill your commitments.

ACTION POINT

Develop a list or database of credible third-party sources for factual information to support the rationale you provide when following up on commitments.

I have a client who runs an executive coaching firm. Some professionals view executive coaching as inherently effective but not very measurable from a performance perspective. My client makes it a point to share specific, third-party, quantitative facts that support the value of executive coaching whenever this aspect surfaces in his sales conversations. This approach has resulted in substantial growth for his firm—but more important, for his reputation as being a man of integrity who his clients can trust.

"Go Ugly" as Early as Possible

We've all experienced that feeling of nervousness deep inside when we come to understand that something we've promised at one price is going to come in well over budget; or when in the middle of pursuing a business opportunity we find that our price needs to be adjusted; or when we realize that our project is headed toward disaster.

At one time in my career I found myself managing a sales organization for one of our subsidiaries. We had made a decision to discontinue supporting a particular database because only a few clients were using it, and it had become too costly for both them and us to use. The salesperson who worked with this client and for whom I was responsible was fearful that we would lose the account completely—so he avoided sharing our decision with them without my knowledge.

Of course, three months down the road I found myself meeting with our CEO, not only sharing how we had failed to notify our client but also that he and I were the guests of honor at a meeting with this very disgruntled client. The meeting turned out to be as challenging as anticipated, and we were barely able to save the account because our credibility and integrity were at an all-time low.

In situations like this one, you have two options:

1. Wait it out, hoping the bad news will somehow disappear or diminish.
2. Face the music as soon as possible, sharing the bad news while you may still be able to do something to compensate for it and before your client blows through their budget.

If you opt to wait it out, you should know that bad news — if ignored — generally gets worse, negatively impacts your reputation, and eventually creates a great deal more consternation than it would if you had addressed the issue before several business cycles had occurred or great sums of money had been spent. Business is sometimes about facing missteps and making adjustments.

Here's where the concept of "going ugly as early as possible" comes into play. Being a Professional Peer who has developed a relationship with a long-range view and is focused on creating relational capital allows your integrity to carry the day, even if the client has to fire you from a particular project. Remember that we can sometimes slide back down a few steps on the Relational Ladder or fall off completely. In a "going ugly early" scenario, the Relational Ladder affords you the opportunity to assess just how far down you might have slipped and to come up with ways to begin advancing the relationship again. In a worst-case scenario, it may reveal that simply getting off the ladder altogether is best for both parties.

ACTION POINT

Anticipate the next instance where you can foresee the need to share some "ugly" information with your client, and then share it.

Doing Business on a Handshake

While I was working at a technology company, I was asked to develop a program to work with key influencers in our market. Corporate America was in the middle of its Y2K anxiety, spending billions on enterprise-wide application software and consulting to make sure everything would work when the clock ticked to 12:00 a.m. on January 1, 2000. Our company was doing well by partnering with the key software vendors in our industry. However, we discovered a gap in our strategy around the Big Six accounting firms. (As you probably know, today this number is down to the Big Four due to consolidation.) We learned that these firms often influenced their clients' software-purchasing decisions, particularly in our area of specialty. We realized that although our company had a good reputation, our salespeople lacked personal connection with the Big Six partners and managers who worked closely with our prospects and customers.

I began thinking about how we could work with these key influencers since our CEO was very committed to partnering to help deliver everything our customers needed. Armed with nothing but his support and my own blind gumption, I set out to meet the key national partners at each firm.

It took many months of meetings, calls, and some important social time together to help these firms understand our true intentions, to build trust, and to prove to them that we were viable partners. At last we were on a roll, working with each firm regarding the best way to partner with us so that their professionals would become expert and certified on our software, leading to potential consulting opportunities for them and positive buying-decision influence for our company.

Life was great, until each firm started talking to its legal department, that is. Now, I have some great friends who are attorneys, so this is no slight to them, but even they would agree that legal departments can really slow down a process.

Apparently, what we were proposing amounted to partnerships, and the whole structure and culture of these firms was based on *being* a partnership — not partnering with others. Rather, they kept everything proprietary, and if they didn't possess a competency, they either built it or went out and bought it.

Time to Get Creative

I suggested to our CEO that since we had earned a great deal of trust with the accounting firms' leaders we should use this quality to everyone's benefit and do business with these firms on a simple handshake. No contracts, no formal agreements.

I went on to explain that it could take years just to reach formal agreement on something as simple as an engagement letter. By that time, we would have missed the Y2K opportunity. I said we had pretty much defined the program and built it so each firm could have its own identity; I felt my relationships with the partners were on solid ground. Convinced, our CEO said, "Why not!"

With another round of meetings to present our radical proposal (during which I had to pick a couple of Big Six partners up off the floor), I assured them that our CEO and I would put our reputations in the industry on the line by personally standing behind the handshake arrangements.

Miraculously, each firm agreed to our concept.

After three years in the program, our company earned significant referral revenue annually and the Big Six consulting practices were each generating several times that amount in revenues from working with our products. To top it off, we were even able to get them all to come together for an annual conference to collaborate on common issues — something previously unheard of in their fiercely competitive environment.

How did this happen?

Certainly, this accomplishment required a lot of one-on-one time talking with the national partners, and lots of time meeting in the various offices of the Big Six practices. It took constant availability to help with questions and conflicts, as well as consistency of judgment when judgment calls were needed. And it required some political savvy to navigate the process, with each firm believing it was the best and competing with the others at every turn.

But behind all that, what really made it possible was our determination to build an environment of fairness, ethics, and trust. We wanted to create an atmosphere of integrity in these relationships where they could trust us as well as each other; we wanted to concentrate on the potential for expanding the size of the pie for all versus the usual concept of everyone fighting for the biggest piece of a limited pie.

To this day, I begin every business relationship with thoughts of worthy intent, which makes it easy to base my own firm's business pursuits and agreements on as many handshakes as are reasonably possible. My clients find it refreshing when I suggest the services our firm will provide, share our fees for the services, and then suggest that we agree by shaking hands—with the services and invoice to follow accordingly.

Displaying integrity and trust is an indispensable ingredient in securing your business relationships. Integrity and trust will significantly help advance your business relationships from the Acquaintance dimension on the Relational Ladder to being regarded as a Professional Peer.

It's simple. Just keep your promises.

RELATIONAL INSIGHTS

☑ Integrity is the foundation of trust and the means to securing your business relationship.

☑ You will display integrity and build trust with your clients by

- Being honest about issues
- Sharing factual information and not opinions
- Setting appropriate commitments and then following through on them
- "Going ugly as early as possible" when bad news needs to be conveyed to the client
- Doing business on a handshake whenever possible to make it easy for you and your clients to work together

Chapter 7

Using Time Purposefully

Everywhere is within walking distance if you have the time!
—Steven Wright, comedian and philosopher

After you have displayed your integrity and built trust by keeping your commitments, the next step up the Relational Ladder
is to "invest in the relationship" through the way you make use
of your client's time and your own time (see figure 7.1). Time is
the most precious resource to both you and your clients. With the
24/7 demands placed on our clients' time today, time is an ally that
offers us an opportunity to distinguish ourselves by the way we go
about effectively using this time when we are together. What better
way to launch into this new chapter than with another anecdote
about business relationship builder par excellence — Max!

168 and Belly Buttons

On yet another trip to the airport, I was a bit detached and Max
commented, "Seems like you're pretty busy today, Ed."

Figure 7.1: Relational Ladder: Using Time Purposefully

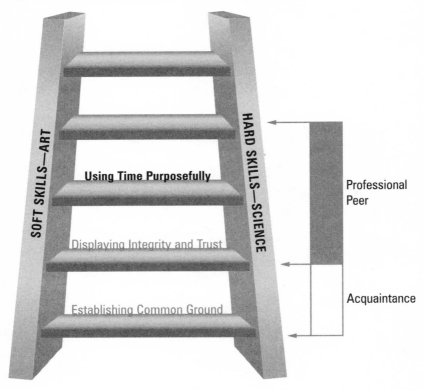

"Oh, sorry, Max. I've got proposals, memos, expense reports — and that's not the half of it. I just can't keep up!" I sighed.

"That's got to be very frustrating. Seems like you're caught in a vicious cycle," he said.

"Right, and that cycle seems endless. Any suggestions?"

Max knew he was on the spot again, but without changing his vocal inflection, he asked, "Do you know anything about the number 168, Ed?"

"168, 168? What's that all about?" I asked.

"Well, think about it," he said. "What could it represent?"

"Max, I'm drowning here, and you're playing paint by numbers with me! Can you at least give me a clue?" I asked frantically.

"Okay. We all have as much in common with the number 168 as we do with having a belly button," Max continued.

168 and belly buttons! Now I'm really *lost,* I thought.

"Think, Ed. Think about *time,* Ed. That's what you're asking about. Think!" he said.

"Time is weeks, days, hours, minutes . . ." I mumbled.

"Hours! Now you're getting warm," Max cheered.

"Hours? There are 24 hours in a day, and I still don't have enough of them."

"Okay, and how many hours are there in a week?"

I thought for a moment. "Aha! 168! Max, you rascal, you could have just told me that right off the bat!"

"Then it may have been too easy, and you might not have recognized the value in knowing that number," he mused.

"I still don't see the value," I said. "We all have a belly button and we all have 168 hours in a week. So what?"

"Precisely. We all have the same amount of time. We also have a great deal of freedom in the ways that we choose to use it, Ed. How do you think the leaders of all the big corporations got to where they are? How did they find the time to do everything that had to be done to make a living, develop new skills, develop relationships, advance their careers, and lead global businesses?"

Max realized that I did not have an answer for him, so he continued. "Well, Ed, I'll tell you," he replied. "They have the same amount of time in the day as you and me, but they choose how to spend their time based on what they want to do, what they believe in. I made a choice to drive a taxi, but in my own way, because I wanted to spend my time in service to my friends. You know, if you *like* what you're doing, you'll never work another day in your life."

After a brief pause, Max continued. "You appear to have chosen to try to squeeze a lot of busy activity into your time. Ever wonder what that activity is really producing?"

What Meeting Time Costs Your Client

In chapter 1 I mentioned the relational blocker *busyness* and contrasted it with conducting valuable business endeavors versus activities. The journey with Max I just recounted was a key inflection point in my career because it got me to start thinking about not only my time but also my clients' time. The principle of worthy intent needed to emerge again as a reminder for me to keep each of my client's best interests at the forefront of our business relationship.

For years I took the act of getting groups of professionals together for meetings as just a part of doing business. But after reflecting on how valuable time can be, I began thinking differently about how I should expect to use my clients' time. Rather than taking for granted their willingness to give up their time for me, I began to think about ways to turn this assumed "cost" into more of an investment for them.

> Rather than take for granted their willingness to give up their time for you, think about ways to turn the cost of that time into an investment.

I zeroed in on all of the meeting time that I was spending with clients and then began thinking about how much of it was actually productive enough to lead to business, versus how much was just ceremonial — what we habitually do to stay in front of the client.

Meetings are as much a part of the fabric of our business day as enjoying coffee at our desks in the morning. We meet to plan meetings, to design processes for future meetings, to discuss a previous meeting, and sometimes because meetings have inexplicably appeared in our calendars. The only problem is that we enjoy the coffee much more than we do the meetings. And if this is true for you, keep in mind it's also true for your clients.

The Ten Most Important Minutes of Your Day

As you move up the Relational Ladder, if you want to sustain your place as a Professional Peer, you need to be concerned about both your own time and that of your client. In fact, stop to think for a minute about how much of your own internal team's time, as well as your client's time, you are seeking for different reasons. Just getting five people together from each team for a two-hour meeting requires a significant commitment from each participant—especially when you add in factors like travel time, transportation, parking, and meals. And don't forget that taking their time to be in your meeting is keeping them from their other priorities. This leads to opportunity costs, which while seldom quantifiable, are predictably expensive, as we all know.

All of the above implies that these interactions are actual expenses and that we should be mindful that our clients likely view our requests for their time in that way. Consequently, this chapter is all about how to ensure, instead, that your clients regard their time spent with you as an investment in a valuable relationship to achieve common objectives.

Many fine professional development programs are available today on time management, personal effectiveness, and improving organizational skills. Therefore, there's no need for me to go into those matters here. But in my experience, there is one particular area where I find client-facing professionals could benefit from some help, and that area is in designing an effective meeting.

ACTION POINT

Think back to recent unproductive meetings that you have attended. What changes would you suggest to make the meeting more effective?

Most meetings are constructed using an itemized list of topics and activities without any time limits or defined meeting roles. Many of my clients share that, due to poor meeting design, sometimes mini-meetings break out within meetings, which turns most of the participants into an audience for the important discussion that two team members are having. Just how productive is that, I ask you?

The ten most important minutes that you can invest prior to a client meeting is thinking through and planning the meeting. I have come up with a series of steps that you can repeat over and over again to help you plan a productive and enjoyable client meeting.

POP

If you guessed that I have an acronym to remind you of the process I want you to remember, you're right. In planning every client meeting I think of POP, which stands for **P**urpose, **O**utcomes, and **P**rocess. These are the three repeatable steps you can use in planning and then collaborating around every single client meeting you will ever schedule. Using POP makes meetings easier to plan and conduct, and it helps you track and follow up on the commitments made during any given meeting.

P Is for Purpose: What and Why   The first step, P, or purpose, involves defining the reasons for the meeting. It answers the "what?" and "why?" aspects of the meeting.

- To describe the specific work to be completed (what)
- To describe the benefits to the participants when the work is completed (why)

Worthy intent plays a key role here: by keeping the group's best interests in the forefront for calling the meeting, it will be easier for you to determine who should attend or whether to even call the meeting.

ACTION POINT

Develop the purpose for a future meeting you are planning to hold. Answer the following questions based on the perceived benefits of the meeting:

What am I trying to accomplish?

Why will the participants benefit?

Do I have the right attendees?

Do I need this many attendees?

Do I need more or less time?

Do I even need to call this meeting?

I mentioned earlier that we hold meetings for many reasons, the least of which is that a meeting was already scheduled, so we might as well hold it. You will save yourself and your client many time cycles when you use a purpose statement to frame upcoming meeting interactions. In fact, you may even rescue everyone's time by not even calling a meeting in the first place!

O Is for Outcomes: Takeaways   By planning the takeaways, O, or outcome(s), that each participant will leave the meeting with, you will best determine who exactly should participate in the meeting. If you invest the time to determine the outcomes up front, then the participant list is much easier to develop. For example, if the purpose for the meeting is to provide an update on a prototype project's status, then you should be able to readily identify the client team members who need this information.

Once you have drafted the intended meeting outcome(s), review it to make sure it supports the "what and why" in the purpose and also the takeaways you desire the participants to leave with. For example:

- Will everyone have a shared understanding of these takeaways?
- Will various participants understand what they need to do (their role, responsibilities, next steps) when the meeting concludes?
- Are the takeaways reasonable, or are they overly ambitious for the time allotted?

Planning your meeting outcomes will save you and your client's team time, help you determine the right mix of professionals to attend the meeting, and continue to distinguish you throughout the process.

P Is for Process: Meeting Agenda   This second P represents the actual steps your meeting will follow to achieve the purpose and outcome(s). The typical meeting agenda includes a list of bulleted discussion points that the participants do not get through because of poor planning and meeting facilitation. The points covered are not always captured and followed up on, while the other points drift about aimlessly in future meetings. The second P in POP takes these meeting discussion points and uses a process to guarantee that they are covered, and appropriately so, within the time allocated.

Here is a sample process for an effective meeting, which lists both the agenda items and the team member(s) responsible for each item on the agenda:

- Update on commitments from previous meeting (meeting leader)
- Introduce specific meeting topic (topic leader)

- Dialogue on topic (group)
- Capture any agreements and/or commitments on the topic (note taker)
- Introduce next meeting topic (topic leader)
- Repeat above dialogue and capture steps
- Arrive at a path forward (meeting leader)
- Close meeting within promised time period (meeting leader)

Let's say it's Monday and your team has an important client meeting scheduled for Thursday afternoon, yet no one has taken responsibility for the meeting plan. One surefire way to earn the respect of your manager and your client is to take ten minutes to use POP to design the meeting. Send the draft process to your client, seeking her input. When the process is finalized, provide all meeting participants with a copy of it.

To help you see how easy it is for you to put this into practice in your workplace, I've reproduced the three steps of a POP I completed for my recent meeting with a membership organization.

ED'S POP FOR VISTAGE INTERNATIONAL

P—Purpose (WHAT are we trying to do and WHY?)

To share the Relational Capital workshop with Vistage International members

So that participants leave with new perspective on advancing their most important business relationships

O—Outcomes (Takeaways)

A repeatable process to identify, assess, and proactively improve the participants' most important business relationships

An Action Plan

P—Process (Agenda)

Introduction and opening exercise (Ed/Group—15 minutes)

Share workshop outline and process (Ed—15 minutes)

Discuss the Essential Qualities of Relational Capital (Ed/Group—30 minutes)

Break (15 minutes)

Relational Ladder exercises (Group—60 minutes)

Summary and follow-up assignments (Ed—10 minutes)

Why can designing a meeting process be so powerful? Think about how your client will receive this help. Think how pleased she will be that you took responsibility for drafting this plan to make the meeting more purposeful, fruitful, and efficient. Think how appreciative she will be that you sought her input in the design process. Think how much more productive the outcomes will be because everyone comes to the meeting prepared and eager to participate.

Because this tool is so important in the context of using your client's time constructively, I have repeated this section's "take-aways" in the form of a summary sheet, which follows. Refer to it often, and use these steps each time you need to "invest" your company's or your client's time and resources in a meeting.

USING TIME PURPOSEFULLY WITH A DYNAMIC POP

Take 10 minutes to plan out your next meeting using POP—Purpose, Outcomes, and Process.

Send the proposed POP to your client and ask for her input in advance of the meeting.

Send out any pre-reading homework, along with the POP, at least 2 days in advance.

Ask one of the participants to take meeting notes on his laptop.

Stay focused on the agreed-upon purpose of the meeting.

Put a "No BlackBerry" rule into effect. This means that participants will get to know each other better during meeting breaks, or they will use the time to network on other issues.

Going Through the Motions

Paul, a client of mine, runs an employee-benefits firm. He recently shared with me that he found himself "just going through the motions" at meetings where he was asked to introduce new programs to his clients' employees. He knew that his audience was hearing about important changes to their plans that would impact their family's health care and finances, yet every presentation he made was simply "routine." I asked Paul to consider using POP to prepare for his next client meeting. He readily agreed because he had a meeting coming up for which his client had specifically asked him to create an agenda that focused on the interaction with employees. Paul took the initiative to develop a meeting plan versus an agenda and share it with his client.

About two weeks later, Paul reported back to me that the client had not only valued the time he had invested in preparing for the meeting but also had seen how committed Paul was to their employee-benefit needs. The client now recommends Paul on a regular basis during the local human resource association meetings, which has led to many new opportunities for Paul's firm. Paul had worked with this client for almost five years but had not secured any referrals until after he began thinking through meetings in advance.

Max mentioned the "little extras." This is a tangible example of a little extra—a demonstration of how by investing in your relationship and honoring your client's time as well as your own, remarkable business performance can result.

Let me conclude this chapter with one final insider's tip about using time purposefully. When you are planning and designing a meeting, consider doing so in a way that you know the meeting will actually end *earlier* than anticipated by your using less time on one of the topics you are presenting. Your clients and colleagues will see and appreciate the importance you're placing on the meeting's value as well as the value of everyone's time. This is always a welcome surprise, and everyone will applaud that outcome!

Using time purposefully is the third step in distinguishing yourself as you develop an outstanding business relationship and move up the Relational Ladder. It solidifies your standing as a Professional Peer, the dimension in which your client or prospect values you professionally and views you as an equal, regardless of your role/level in the business relationship.

> Everywhere is within walking distance if you make the time.

RELATIONAL INSIGHTS

☑ Time is your client's most precious resource, and the way you use your client's time will become a distinguishing attribute in your relationship.

☑ You will continue your ascent up the Relational Ladder through "investing in the relationship" by focusing on something as commonplace as your next business meeting.

☑ Turn this assumed cost into an investment in the relationship by taking ten minutes to use the POP—**P**urpose, **O**utcomes, and **P**rocess—approach to plan for an effective meeting.

☑ The POP approach can be used for any type of meeting to ensure that everyone knows what the meeting is about, why they need to attend, and what takeaways they will leave with.

Chapter 8

Offering Help

Significance comes from helping others.
—*Lou Holtz*

Moving up the Relational Ladder is a continual process of taking actions and making observations about each individual business relationship you're involved in. Specifically, I'm talking about actions you and your client take and observations you make regarding your client's behaviors. The previous two chapters emphasized the importance of advancing most of your business relationships into the Professional Peer dimension. At this step on the ladder, you will want to advance no more than 10 percent of those relationships into an even higher dimension, that of Respected Advisor.

Respected Advisors

Once you have clearly displayed integrity in a business relationship and earned a person's trust, the path is clear for you to be even more authentic, to feel completely comfortable being you.

Authenticity—in other words, simply being yourself—goes hand in hand with advancing to the highest dimension of relationship on the Relational Ladder. Being authentic is essential if you are to emerge from being a Professional Peer with a client to being perceived and treated as a Respected Advisor (see figure 8.1).

Respected Advisors work at such a high level that their relationships transcend business aspects and carry over to personal friendships. Respected Advisor relationships are equally challenging and rewarding because your client seeks your advice and opinions not only on matters related to your ordinary sphere of business activity but also on issues and decisions *outside* of the

Figure 8.1: Relational Ladder: Offering Help

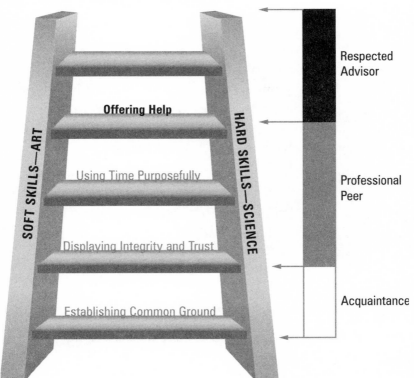

original business reason or issue that brought you together. A Respected Advisor's opinions are likewise valuable to you. When you are able to ask each other such questions as "What is your opinion of . . . ?" "How do you think we should . . . ?" and "Can you refer someone who . . . ?" you know you have achieved a high degree of comfort with one another.

You may recall that I suggested that at the Acquaintance dimension on the Relational Ladder your client does not want your help. In fact, offering help may even work against you at that early stage in the relationship. However, once you've secured and invested in the relationship by establishing true credibility and displaying trust, your client will be open to the idea of accepting your help. At this point, you are in a prime position to grow the relationship by offering help on existing as well as anticipated challenges.

Who's Authentic?

One exercise I use during the "Offering Help" segment of my workshops is to ask clients to name a businessperson they believe is truly authentic. Normally, what follows is a very long pause because this request is more challenging than it appears. Eventually, responses trickle in and include Howard Schultz and Richard Branson and, most often, Herb Kelleher from Southwest Airlines, who is as genuine a leader as you will find. I like to add to the list a lesser-known but nonetheless effective CEO, Tom Feeney, who runs Safelite AutoGlass, a large division of Belron, Inc.

Tom has always been focused on the importance of relationships in his company. In fact, he is one of those leaders in the "less than 5 percent" category I mentioned earlier who actually has strategies and processes in place to advance business relationships. His worthy intentions and authenticity are evident in the way he goes about his work. One story goes that while Tom was visiting a Safelite store that he knew to be struggling, he noticed an Enterprise

Leasing branch across the street. He decided to go ask the branch manager why he was not a Safelite customer.

Tom simply walked across the street and asked the manager if he was interested in working with Safelite because they had some new programs for businesses like Enterprise. Tom never explained that he was the CEO; he just allowed his worthy intentions to carry the day. The branch manager was so pleased with Tom's genuine approach that he agreed to begin working with the local Safelite store for all of his windshield repair needs.

The moral of this story, in Tom's own words, is: "Business opportunities are everywhere, even in a down market. All you have to do is look, and sometimes they are right next door."

My favorite phrase to describe authenticity is "You'll know it when you see it." That's Tom Feeney!

Worthy Intent in the Respected Advisor Dimension

Offering help requires some real thought and relational savvy. People have all kinds of ways to assess and discern whether your intentions are genuine, so it's important to be clear about your motives. When you consider offering help to someone, it's a good idea to pause and ask yourself, "Why am I doing this?" Your answer should be that you are doing it with the client's best interest in mind. You should never offer help in order to impress a client, to earn points, or to set a client up for a request that will help you instead.

> When you consider offering help to someone, pause and ask yourself, "Why am I doing this?" You should be doing it with the client's best interest in mind.

From both a business and a personal perspective, having worthy intent when offering help can serve to advance your relationship from the Professional Peer into the Respected Advisor dimension.

As your business relationship moves toward the Respected Advisor dimension, you will notice that your client is open to your unsolicited offers of help. You will both begin to experience the following behaviors:

- Seeking unrelated advice outside the scope of the original reason that brought you together
- Including each other in one another's planning processes
- Providing early warning signals when issues surface
- Referring each other personally and initiating the contact at a peer or higher level

ACTION POINT

Reflect on your best business relationships and determine whether your client is exhibiting any of the previous behaviors. If not, then your relationship may not be as strong as you believe.

As you experience these behaviors, you will recognize that your clients may need your help in both their business lives and their personal lives.

Business Life

A client's business life encompasses a great range of priorities and pursuits. Depending on the nature of the relationship, your particular product, service, or area of expertise may occupy only a very small portion of any given client's business time or interest. It would be unreasonable to expect all your clients to be thinking about you and your "stuff" all the time, but your hope is to at least occupy a respectable position on their list.

Once you realize and accept that your client has other things going on in his professional life—just as you do—try to also realize that this fact can constitute your best opportunity to help this person. To do this, first take a few moments to think about what it would be like to walk in his shoes. Imagine the other areas of concern that probably make up this person's Relational GPS and occupy his time. Here are a few likely candidates for such a list:

- Your client's company—reputation, values, industry position, competitive environment
- His company's performance
- His own role and status in the organization
- His relationship with his manager

Second, ask yourself, "If I were this person, what, specifically, might be keeping me up at night?" If you've gotten to know this contact as well as required at this stage of developing the relationship, you're likely to have some very good ideas. Please write these down. They may be similar to the following:

- My company is growing almost too rapidly.
- My company is struggling financially.
- I am feeling overburdened with multiple projects.
- My projects are contributing to this burden.

Now think about how you might be able to offer real help in a scenario like one of these. What if, for example, you see the business environment changing and you believe that some of the dynamics may seriously impact this client. You know that you're in a high-level Professional Peer business relationship and that you're edging toward the status of Respected Advisor.

The urgency of the situation—and your conviction that you can help—may lead you to go a step beyond where you have previously been with this person. You might go directly to them and say something like the following:

> Joe, I've been thinking about your situation and what I know about the challenges you're facing this year. I was wondering, would it be helpful for us to review the timing on the different projects we have in the works and explore ways to relieve some of the scheduling pressure?

This is one of those step-back-and-get-smarter moments. While your own goals may be pushed out a bit, what is the price if one of those projects that you are jamming in fails or creates big changes in the project for Joe? It's likely that your relational capital would take a negative hit, and as a consequence, you would slide back down the Relational Ladder.

ACTION POINT

Offer help to a contact in your network who could do the least for you, but with a small amount of attention, you could do the most for them.

As Professional Peers, you and Joe are working in very effective ways: collaborating, problem solving, and focusing on immediate issues. You're also focused on what you can do to grow the relationship for mutual benefit. As a result, his likely response to your question will be one of interest and appreciation. Your collaboration will continue, with a net gain for you both in the evolving relationship.

Bottom line, if your client is receptive to your offer for help, you are moving toward Respected Advisor status.

ACTION POINT

Think about a client who could greatly benefit from an introduction you could make on their behalf. Make the introduction without any expectation for them to reciprocate.

Clients Will Seek Your Opinion   Another kind of opportunity to offer help comes in the form of questions from your contact, often relating to issues beyond the realm of your existing relationship or your specific offerings as a businessperson. As I mentioned earlier, these requests may start with phrases like the following:

- What do you think about . . . ?
- What is your opinion of . . . ?
- We're looking to fill a new position; can you recommend anyone?
- I'm thinking about promoting Jackie. How do you think she'd do in that position?

These types of inquiries indicate that your client now views you as a critical business partner.

At this stage, you have a tremendous advantage over the competitors who have not achieved this relationship status, and you are also now in a position to begin to grow the relationship further. You have transcended merely providing valuable offerings and pricing on a consistent basis and have become a Respected Advisor. As your relational capital increases in intensity, the questions you are asked stray farther from the scope of areas addressable by your offerings alone.

After you've provided authentic help in response to client questions, the relationship continues to advance toward the top of the Relational Ladder. A word of caution: Even though it's flattering to be asked these types of questions, there is power in the phrase "I don't know" or in saying that you don't feel you are the best person to provide guidance on this matter. Trying to provide advice in areas where you lack expertise will ultimately deplete your relational capital. (In chapter 9 you will learn more about the power of saying "I don't know," as well as about your right to ask for a client's help.)

ACTION POINT

Reflect on recent interactions when your client has asked your opinion about something outside the scope of your existing business relationship.

Personal Life

Respected Advisors get to know about each other's personal lives as well as their business lives. This is where you start to become friends, just as Max did with his taxicab riders. When you feel a client is unwilling to share much about their personal common ground or the passions element of their Relational GPS, continue serving them at a Professional Peer level. Most often, however, your clients will be receptive to sharing on a personal level.

Clients will usually be open to sharing basic information about their private lives. This is the type of information most client-facing professionals have in their CRM systems: professional experience, education, current professional position, and trade associates.

When clients share these aspects, it is an indication that you and the client have a healthy Professional Peer relationship. However, when clients open up and share information about any of the following, you can be assured that you are Respected Advisors: family members, life goals, passions, struggles, hobbies, attitude toward their employer, and career plans (whether they will remain at their job, transfer, or retire).

Each of these categories and aspects has the potential to provide opportunities for you to be helpful. You might find out that your client's daughter is interested in applying to a school where you have valuable contacts. Perhaps one of your clients confides in you that she has some discomfort working under a new management team, and you would be able to confidentially offer advice from your own experience, or refer her to another colleague who could help.

I have some friends in the insurance business who have built their reputations on the concept of completely getting to know their clients on a personal level. They take an interest in their clients' families, remember birthdays, forward articles of special interest with a personal note, attend family celebrations, and so on. They use their intense love of sports as a basis to develop and maintain relationships with their clients who are sports fans — attending games and hosting sports-themed parties. They maintain a Client Profile database in their CRM system with three simple categories: Client Background, Business Background, and Special Interests, which includes areas of client interest and concern. They gather this information on every client and continually update and make use of it because they know how important this part of their relationship development approach is to making their business successful. Figure 8.2 shows an abstract of the client profile they maintain.

I marvel at this list: besides the standard required client demographic information, it includes specifics like client's nickname, information about the client's family, and even areas usually avoided in business, such as the client's religious affiliation. While gathering some of this information may not work "politically" in some industries, in the insurance business, really getting to know someone at a personal level is paramount to maintaining the business relationship. It can also lead to additional Relational GPS knowledge that allows the client-facing professional to offer clients expanded opportunities to help.

Figure 8.2: Abstract of Client Profile

Client Background	Business Background
Name	Previous employment
Nickname	Company
Title	Location
Company name	How long?
Address	Title
Phone numbers	Professional or trade association
Birth date	Client's attitude toward company
Birthplace	Client's business objectives
Hometown	**Special Interests**
College	
Special degrees	Clubs
High school	Political party
Extracurricular activities	Religion
Military service? Y N	Favorite places to eat
Marital status	Hobbies and recreational interests
Spouse's name	Reading interests
Spouse's education	Sports interests
Spouse's interests	Vacation preferences
Children's names and ages	Additional notes
Children's schools	
Children's interests	

You can use this client profile template to create your own, personalizing it with additional inquiry points to really get to know your own clients. Of course, you can expand or limit a client's profile to fit your needs, but my suggestion would be to include as much information as possible.

ACTION POINT

After reviewing the client profile, think about one of your Fab 5—that is, your five most important business relationships. How many of the prompts can you answer about that person? For clients for whom you know fewer than ten of the answers (discounting name and address), spend some additional time getting to know them better.

Max's Journey Out of the Middle East

As you really get to know your clients at a personal level, you will also begin to share much more about yourself and your own Relational GPS. For example, after many rides together, Max began to realize that I was taking very seriously a lot of the things he was saying. I was relatively young and impressionable, so one day Max turned to me and said, "Ed, you know I really enjoy our conversations. But I hope you're making your own careful decisions on the matters we discuss."

"I don't mean to put you on the spot, but your advice has been important to me," I replied.

"It's okay," he said. "Let's make a deal. From here on out, I'll keep that in mind and maybe I can be more of a mentor to you, since a mentor helps you find your own truth rather than imposing his truth on you. How's that work for you?"

Of course, I was more than happy to agree.

Max knew that I found it remarkable that he had so much corporate business savvy from running a seemingly simple taxi business. He shared with me that before he started driving his taxicab, he had trained as an engineer and had a career as an executive working for a large oil company. In fact, in the late 1970s he had accepted an important assignment to work in the Middle East. Unfortunately, his assignment also coincided with the Iran hostage crisis in 1979 in which sixty-six American diplomats and civilians were taken captive in the U.S. Embassy, a situation that dragged on for fourteen months, bedeviled the Carter administration, and cast a long shadow over U.S. foreign affairs. It was an extremely challenging and dangerous time to be an American working in the Middle East.

By that time Max had learned a variety of strategies for developing relationships as well as the protocols for survival, for communication, for looking out for others in the community, and for managing the day-to-day logistics of living and working under hostile conditions. He had had to become an expert, not only in his original field of business but also in the cultural, political, and economic realities that dominated every aspect of life there at that time. Talk about balancing your hard and soft skills!

But at one point before the crisis escalated, Max's Iranian friends notified him that he needed to leave before more serious steps were taken. At that point, Max had had enough of the politics, pressure, danger, stress, and anxiety. He thought hard and deeply about what was important in his life, and he began to reorganize his priorities. He and his family moved back to the United States. He desired to live a simple life of service to people, taking the lessons he had learned about human nature, relationships, and life and applying and sharing them freely. This was the point at which he purchased a British taxi and set up his business providing rides, wisdom, and friendship.

Through our friendship, Max told me he had found not only another friend but also someone who valued and understood his philosophy about business relationships, someone he could authentically share it with in the hopes that it would continue to benefit others in some small way. Now I knew some essential things about Max that I hadn't known before, which put our relationship on a much more authentic basis. Who knew that I would one day write this book and Max would be the central character to help us all learn how to develop outstanding business relationships?

By offering authentic help to our clients, we *"share the equity"* that comes from the relational capital we have created in our business relationship. Respected Advisors work at a very authentic level, where their offers of help are not only valued but anticipated. Continuing to do business together is foundational and never in question as you advance your relationship up the Relational Ladder.

> As in opportunities to offer help in someone's business life, when a client values your help in a personal matter, you can be certain you have become Respected Advisors.

RELATIONAL INSIGHTS

☑ Respected Advisor is the highest dimension in the Relational Ladder, where your advice is sought on your client's goals, passions, and struggles beyond the original issues that brought you together.

☑ This dimension is difficult to reach and requires ongoing relational investment to sustain.

☑ The initial business aspects of your relationship are secure and new opportunities emerge.

☑ Authenticity is the operative quality at this level, where being your genuine self allows for stronger relational bonds.

☑ Offers of help to your clients on their business and personal goals, passions, and struggles are valued and encouraged.

Chapter 9

Asking for Help

There are three things extremely hard: steel, a diamond, and to know one's self.
—Benjamin Franklin

We've just discussed how, in advancing up the Relational Ladder, you go into the relationship with worthy intent, work to establish credibility and trust, and then you earn opportunities to be your authentic self with your business contacts by offering your help. When you reach the point where your client is receptive to your offer for help, you know you are moving from the role of Professional Peer into the dimension of being a Respected Advisor (see figure 9.1).

But the authenticity required to successfully make this important transition involves more than the offering of help. It involves being able to *ask for help* as well—being authentic and courageous enough to demonstrate that you don't have all of the answers.

Figure 9.1: Relational Ladder: Asking for Help

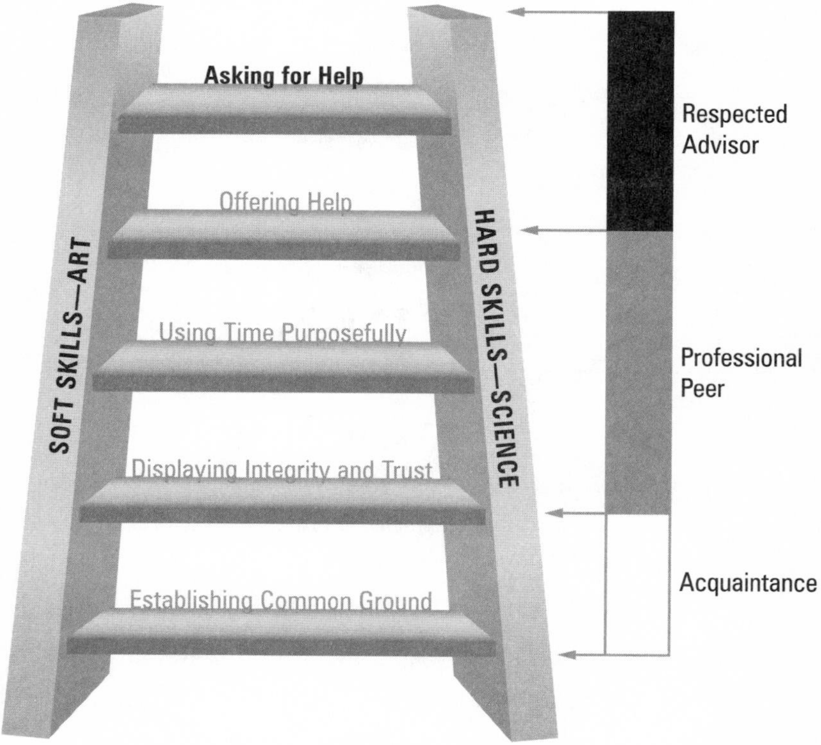

Asking for Help

Offering Help

Using Time Purposefully

Displaying Integrity and Trust

Establishing Common Ground

SOFT SKILLS—ART

HARD SKILLS—SCIENCE

Respected Advisor

Professional Peer

Acquaintance

Intellectual Honesty

Too often, businesspeople put a lot of energy into keeping up a façade in their business relationships — an appearance of strength, expertise, influence, or success — for fear that others will see them as weak or vulnerable. However, I've found that when I feel free and comfortable just to be who I am — to be authentically me, without embellishment or hype — people tend to believe, trust, and respect me, and we make more progress in whatever challenge stands before us. When we are honest with ourselves about our own capabilities and intelligence then this becomes a positive relational attribute we can put to work in building trusted relationships with our clients.

A great example of intellectual honesty is manifested by the approach my friend Lauren uses. She runs a large and successful sales and services organization that brings technology solutions to large corporate clients. Lauren cannot possibly know every detail of her clients' projects and how her clients view her team. She just "does not know." So every quarter Lauren sets up a meeting with each client and simply asks, "How are we doing?"

> Intellectual honesty is rare air these days.

Her authenticity in seeking each client's help in understanding various aspects of the work they are delivering is viewed positively, not only by her clients but also by her client-facing teams. It is not surprising then that Lauren is in line to succeed the CEO after he retires. Intellectual honesty is rare air these days.

ACTION POINT

Think about three clients that are using your products and services. Make it a point to ask them, "How are we doing?"

"I Don't Know"

Three of the scariest words in business are *I don't know*. Saying them, we feel, would make us vulnerable to harsh judgment from our peers, managers, and clients. One aspect of being true to yourself, however, means being able to admit—to yourself and to others— that you are vulnerable. We have been conditioned to view lack of knowledge as a weakness, so voluntarily admitting to this, instead of winging it through a situation, may seem counterintuitive.

However, just the opposite is true: It takes more strength to say "I don't know" than it does to pretend we know what we don't.

I learned that a big turning point in anyone's career is being able to admit this to yourself and others, no longer needing to "fake it until you make it," as the saying goes. One of the hardest things for client-facing professionals, especially as they are trying to move up the Relational Ladder, is to admit openly that they don't have all the answers. Ironic though it may seem, saying "I don't know" can open the doors to a healthy discussion about possible solutions and resources that could lead to an answer. The fact that the individual may be admitting that he or she isn't the ultimate source of wisdom on the matter in question is not relevant; what is relevant is that everyone is able to focus on the need itself and how to meet it most effectively, together.

The willingness to say you don't know everything is, in a way, the opening to have a constructive collaboration with a client. It moves you out of the mode of having everything figured out in advance, which can be off-putting and can signal that you have not really been listening to the other person or taking his or her unique needs into consideration.

Getting to "I don't know" is an essential step toward reaching the third phase in the evolving sales process we saw in figure 2.2. It is moving past the mere transactional-based approach, becoming more service oriented, and finally, functioning in a true collaborative, tailored, problem-solving partnership with the client.

ACTION POINT

Think back to the last time you communicated to your client that you did not have the answer. How did you present this, what resulted, and what would you have done differently?

Why Are Fourth Graders Braver Than We Are?

To illustrate the power of "I don't know" at its simplest level, here's an example from my own experience. I witnessed an amazing phenomenon in my son's fourth-grade class during Observation Day. The teacher was going over some math problems that were challenging—at least to me. Yet the kids were absolutely fearless in their attempts to answer each question. They had no anxiety over possible failure or what the others thought of them—only enthusiasm to attempt the challenge. They embraced the magic words "I don't know" and simply relished the task of finding the right answer. How easy is that?

Yet, we've all been in a meeting where an executive drones on in a presentation, and the eyes of everyone in the room have glazed over and are just barely following the words on each slide. (Picture actor Ben Stein with his dry, monotone delivery giving a presentation.) As adults, we're often afraid of the dynamics, the politics of the people in the room. We're afraid of what others would think of us, or what might happen to our jobs, if we said something that implied we didn't totally comprehend everything being presented.

Of course, having the honesty and authenticity to say "I don't follow you" or "I'm not sure I understand" not only creates healthy and creative collaborations with prospects and clients, it also leads to customized solutions and repeat business. Furthermore, it can lead to encouraging other kinds of important help, such as asking a client for referrals to other potential clients, which is the topic of the next section.

The End of Cold-calling

During a recent discussion about cold calls, David, a client and chief marketing officer of a large public company, shared the following with me:

> When I get a cold call, the chances are one in a thousand that I will have a need or be remotely interested in the caller's offering. But when someone calls me who is referred by a friend or a business colleague or someone else with whom I have a relationship, I am going to take the call because of my relationship with the person who referred them. I don't want my relationship with them to atrophy.

David's comments support the mountain of research that indicates your chances for a meeting or a conversation with a prospective client increase dramatically when you are referred by a client, business colleague, or friend.

A Business Built on Blind Dating

Whenever I address large groups of client-facing professionals, I enjoy telling the story of my friends Marty, Jay, and Bill, who run a mortgage and financial services firm. Their business success story not only conveys the impact of referrals—or blind dating, as they call it—but also serves as a powerful example of why an intentional focus on creating relational capital leads to high-performing business relationships.

The compelling fact about this firm is that its business depends entirely on referrals, which means it's based totally on the quality of their relationships. Their actual customers are bankers, lawyers, and accountants who work regularly with small and medium-sized businesses. Sometimes, these businesses encounter difficulties—such as credit problems, a lawsuit, or impending foreclosure—where standard types of financing aren't available to them, and their banker, lawyer, or accountant has to refer them to a specialty firm for help. It's my friends' goal to maintain such good relations with these three groups that they are the referral they think of first.

From the start, my friends recognized that knowing the referring client intimately was the key to their success. The hardest part of their business, however, would be to get this client to provide a referral. This is because when the bank's or lawyer's own reputation and relationships are at stake, they need to know that they are sending their customer to a company they fully trust to treat people fairly and honestly and to solve the problem effectively.

If you ask him about this challenge, Bill authentically says: "In our business, people can exist without us. We have a good service to provide, but there are others providing the same service, so our job is to get the client to think of us and to send us the business because they like the way we treat their customer."

Marty expresses it differently as he reflects on his earlier days: "Asking someone to send you a customer on trust is like asking them to set you up with a blind date. It has to be someone they have a high regard for. They have to think, 'Who am I going to send on a date with this person? Who can I trust to really come through and not disappoint or embarrass me?' You have to get to that point in developing the relationship."

My friends also feel a real sense of responsibility and commitment—dare I say worthy intent?—in service to their clients. Jay shared that there are times when their relational capital with the lender, the title companies, and sometimes even the IRS buys a "few extra days" to close a complicated loan before foreclosure or tax seizure.

Jay emphasizes that they have saved untold businesses and personal livelihoods from disaster by doing what has to be done, though some people they help have no real sense of how much the firm has saved them. He said, "It's like when a kid walks out on thin ice on a pond and you manage to pull him back before he falls through; they don't know the danger they were in and may or may not even thank you for it until sometime down the road."

One thing is certain, however. They would never succeed — with the banks or with the small businesses that come to them for help — if they were not experts at developing their own brand of relational capital. With the time, effort, and sincerity they invest in these relationships, every banker, lawyer, and accountant who continues to refer business, every friend who they keep in business, and every laugh they have with a client contributes to building the reserves of trust, goodwill, and friendship that are the foundation of everything they have accomplished. They are doing remarkable things in a commoditized business for business owner friends in need of help through understanding the value of relationships.

Now let's take a closer look at business referrals using the familiar model of a social blind date that Marty suggests. In our personal lives, prior to eHarmony the idea of blind dating involved someone setting up a date between two of his friends who had previously not met. Think about the kind of person you would select to set up a blind date for a friend you greatly respected and admired. You would probably select someone who you

- Like
- Trust not to embarrass you or your friend
- Believe is credible
- Share common interests with
- Know shares the same values, challenges, or objectives as your friend

In short, you wouldn't set up two people only because they were single; you would try to ensure that the date would be a good experience for both parties. Business referrals are very similar to blind date setups because the referring person has the worthy intent to help both parties, knows them to be credible and unlikely to embarrass him, and truly believes the connection will help each party with one of their goals, passions, or struggles.

As you move up the Relational Ladder and become Professional Peers and Respected Advisors, you should have more and more opportunities to seek referrals from your clients. Think about how much easier a call is when you can mention that someone you know — a business or a personal friend — referred you. Confidence is an overarching driver when it comes to successful prospecting. Just like in golf, if you believe that you can make the putt, the odds seem to increase that you will.

During workshops, I typically see a room full of blank stares when I suggest that cold calling be made completely obsolete in the sales process. But as I emphasized in chapter 7 about using time purposefully, think about how important it is to both you and the potential clients you are contacting that you spend your prospecting time performing only those activities that are most likely to be successful.

ACTION POINT

Imagine that you work for my friend Jerry's box business and rank your confidence level (high, medium, or low) in each of the following scenarios:

Cold Call—You do not know the business contact

"Hi, Bill, my name is Ed Wallace, and I noticed your trucks driving around town. It would seem that you are a candidate for some of our boxes."

Passive Referral—You are permitted to use the referring person's name

"Hello, Bill, I was referred to you by Charles Gordon, your accountant, who I have known for many years. He shared that it could be beneficial for you and me to get together to discuss your packaging needs."

Direct Referral—The person referring you makes the initial contact

Charles, the accountant, contacts Bill and personally introduces you prior to your outreach to Bill via e-mail or in person.

Which approaches should logically work best? Which approaches would you be more confident in taking forward? With which approach do you believe you would be more successful in having Bill take your call or set up a meeting with you?

Obtaining a Referral

Just how do you go about asking for a referral? First, reflect on where your business relationship stands on the Relational Ladder. Remember when we were talking about the initial meeting ROC (building **R**apport, sharing the meeting **O**bjectives, and developing **C**redibility) process, I asked you to think about how to find a common ground basis for a relationship? Well, the same thinking applies to asking for your client's help and referrals.

We have seen that offering and asking for help early on in a business relationship, when you are still in the Acquaintance dimension, will not likely lead to success and might group you with all the other indistinguishable client-facing professionals. However, as Professional Peers and Respected Advisors, you're much more likely to be successful asking for referrals — and even getting them without asking.

If your assessment of your client's behaviors and the results you have to date is that you are perceived by him as either a Professional Peer or a Respected Advisor, then two options are open to you for how you might go about seeking a referral. Notice that the act of *asking for help* occurs in both versions.

- **Formal version**: "Joe, we've worked together for many years, and you've mentioned on more than one occasion that you're very pleased with our business relationship. I was wondering if you would consider helping me with an introduction to Joan at ABC?"
- **Informal version**: "Joe, can I ask your help with a referral to Joan over at ABC?"

ACTION POINT

Draft a formal and an informal request to generate new referrals for your business.

Performance Is Proof

What I'm about to share is an example of just how powerful seeking referrals can be. My friend Jerry and I spent some time analyzing all of his company's best business relationships. We determined that each of his forty-two client-facing professionals had at least three Professional Peer or Respected Advisor relationships. Jerry then asked each to abandon cold calling for three months and, instead, to ask for five referrals from each of their Professional Peer and Respected Advisor relationships.

Do you recall how I've repeatedly asserted in this book that "business relationships that last" result in real, measurable business performance? Well, here's the proof. Jerry's sales team's initiative resulted in an average of fifteen referrals per client-facing professional—totaling more than six hundred higher-potential candidates for follow-up meetings. Since participating in this exercise, morale among Jerry's client-facing professionals has increased markedly and actual new business from referrals has increased 74 percent.

Respected Advisor Relationships

Respected Advisor relationships have dynamics outside of the original business challenge that brought the parties together. Respected Advisors converse with one another sharing personal challenges as easily and naturally as they do business objectives. The concept of continuing to do business is always assumed. Respected Advisors ask each other questions similar to the following:

- "What do you think about the impact of this development on my business?"
- "What's your opinion of this staffing change?"
- "Can you share how you went about searching for a university for your daughter?"

Respected Advisors regularly send each other on unsolicited blind date referrals. Each partner's voicemail and inbox now include opportunities that are both pleasant and unexpected. So when you find yourself experiencing these kinds of interactions with your client, you know that you are at the top of the Relational Ladder.

In the Respected Advisor dimension, the solid, long-term viability of the partnership, and the referrals your client and friend now freely shares with you, constitute the tangible, bankable—and well-deserved—returns on the persistent, careful, and sincere investment you have made in the relationship over time.

I mentioned that your client's behaviors are indicators of where you are as you advance up the Relational Ladder. Figure 9.2 shows the subtle differences between Professional Peers and Respected Advisors.

Figure 9.2: Comparison of the Professional Peer/ Respected Advisor Dimensions

Professional Peers	Respected Advisors
Share business goals, passions, and struggles	Share business and personal goals, passions, and struggles
Begin to share some personal confidences	Include you in their strategic planning processes and provide early warning signs on issues
Share aspects of their strategies	
Value your time as much as their own	Ask for your help in areas outside of the original scope of your business relationship
Will refer you upon request	Initiate unsolicited referrals on your behalf

Respected Advisor relationships are probably what you had in mind when you went into business in the first place. I know that was certainly the case in my own experience. You have by now realized the significant returns from your continued investment in the business relationship. You and your client experience a mutual respect for each other's time, and your credibility and integrity are at high enough levels so you are each willing to refer or act as a reference for the other.

It's Not Prospecting, It's Building Relationships!

At one point in my career I took a corporate sales position with a major corporation. I had a pretty decent first year, but partway into the second year, my boss (Jim Mullen, who is now my business partner) stopped by my office one day. Now, Jim was not a hard-driving sales manager; he was more of a Father Flanagan counselor type. He asked how I thought things were going. This was his way of opening a conversation about how my performance was slipping (my sales were well behind quota) without coming right out and saying, "Ed, your sales are off."

I answered, "Jim, I keep working harder and harder, but my sales aren't improving. In fact, they're getting worse."

"Seems like you need to think about how you are going about things, Ed. Sometimes it's not just what you do, it's also how you do it!" he said.

We agreed that I would come back to him with some thinking on this problem and that we'd work together on a plan to improve my performance.

So I thought about how client-facing professionals spend their time. We look for commonalities with the buyer. We try to distinguish ourselves from the competition. We all prospect, we all have a sales cycle, and we all have a contract to get signed. We all try to make a monthly quota.

I began looking for another approach, some way to be distinctive and more effective. I thought about this for weeks. Jim was getting a bit anxious because *his* boss was getting a bit anxious.

Finally, one day I looked at my prospect list and asked myself the same question about each one: "Would he consider buying on the twenty-fourth of the month instead of the thirty-first?" I thought through all of them and was able to answer yes for about half of the list.

I realized that I had been caught up in the same process and timing that my prospects were caught up in. They needed to make buying decisions at the same time that salespeople like me had to close business. It made for a chaotic time during that last week of every month. Inevitably, I had to give away value in the crunch, and my clients weren't always completing all of their ordering on time either. I decided to ask Jim for his help with a new approach.

I sat down with Jim and asked for his support with a strategy that created an internal deadline for me by the twenty-fourth of every month rather than the end of the month. He blinked, since he had been at this for many years and had never heard of this approach before. Eventually, he okayed the plan, but only for one quarter, and with one condition that would ultimately make or break my success with this approach: I had to be authentic enough with my prospects *to ask each one for their help*.

I asked Jim, "Why would I ever ask prospects for help?"

Jim said, "Ed, you have created great relationships with your prospects and have earned the right to ask for their help. Plus, asking for help implies friendship, and friends help each other!"

Jim knew that this would do more than help me qualify my prospects. He knew that the act of asking for help would put human nature to work in my favor, because most people genuinely want to help others, even more so when they really care about you as a person and value the relationship. If they care about you as a person and if they value the relationship, then they want you to succeed.

Armed with Jim's support, I set out to contact each prospect who was close to a buying decision and ask for his or her help with my idea of closing business earlier each month. After a few months, I was rolling. My orders were coming in by the third week of every month, our production people had more time to get their end-of-month orders processed, and customers were receiving their orders sooner. Now I was able to be out doing what I enjoyed best—*building relationships*—while my competitors were still trying to prospect and close business. I felt I was always a few days to a week ahead of the pack—a very rewarding feeling, indeed. And guess what? That year, my telesales rep and I had the number one–producing territory for our company, which led to the Sales Team of the Year award.

Upon reflection, I can trace this success to two dynamics:

1. The ability to acknowledge that I did not have all the answers
2. The inherent desire in people to help each other

Asking for help is a very powerful request and a major benefit of building deep business relationships that last. If you are not asking for help from time to time, then why are you working on business relationships at all? Whether you get help or not will determine right then and there whether you have developed an outstanding business relationship.

Now you have experienced the 5 Steps to Transform Contacts into High-Performing Relationships that are involved in the process of moving up the Relational Ladder. To review, they are

Establishing Common Ground
Displaying Integrity and Trust
Using Time Purposefully
Offering Help
Asking for Help

Next I'll introduce a more scientific methodology, called RQ, to help you measure where you actually stand on the Relational Ladder with any given individual, and show you how to systematically advance to the next dimension. You will then use this information and analysis to complete your very first Action Plan so you can get busy advancing your relational capital with every business contact you meet.

Becoming a Respected Advisor is the culmination of climbing each step of the Relational Ladder. It results in an outstanding two-way relationship—especially when you and your client become friends!

RELATIONAL INSIGHTS

☑ The Respected Advisor dimension is where each person's advice is sought on issues and decisions outside of the original business reason that brought them together.

☑ Respected Advisors realize significant returns on their relationship investment when their clients refer them personally to other business associates.

☑ Intellectual honesty involves being able to ask for help—being authentic and courageous enough to demonstrate that you don't have all the answers.

☑ Saying "I don't know" can open the doors to a healthy discussion about possible solutions and resources that could lead to even better solutions.

☑ Respected Advisors understand each other's Relational GPS—goals, passions, and struggles—and share them regularly.

PART THREE

Action Planning

Chapter 10

Discovering Your RQ

Curiosity has its own reason for existing.
—Albert Einstein

One of the promises I made at the beginning of this book was that you would be able to develop an Action Plan to apply what you learned to your existing client opportunities. Now that you understand the benefits of worthy intent and the impact that the three essential qualities have as you move through the five steps of the Relational Ladder process, you can focus on your Action Plan. Before you take that step, however, consider how much more effective that plan would be if there were an approach to measure the quality and value of the business relationships in your Action Plan. I have developed just such an approach, which I call the RQ Assessment, to quantify this value by measuring your relational intelligence (RQ) and, ultimately, to help you create concrete strategies that will allow you to complete your Action Plan for advancing up the Relational Ladder.

To begin, think back to chapter 2 where I asked you to reflect on your goals and objectives for the next twelve months and to come up with (write down) the names of your Fab 5, the five most important business relationships, new or existing, that you need to cultivate in order to achieve those objectives. You will likely have more than five such business relationships, but I like to use a manageable number that will further help you internalize the concepts, develop your Action Plan, and get started immediately. The same process can be applied to all of your business relationships going forward.

Now that you have learned a great deal more about creating relational capital, please review your Fab 5 and your objectives and consider whether this list is still on-target. If you did not complete this step earlier, now is a great time to do so because your Fab 5 will be at the heart of your Action Plan.

Please consider including key existing client or targeted future relationships in your industry and/or business community that are closely tied to your objectives and business networking needs. A relationship with your manager, a business-level peer, and someone who reports to you are also strong candidates for your Fab 5 list since the achievement of some goals may rest with the advancement of these relationships. Thinking about your objectives and then identifying the important business relationships you need to advance and achieve these objectives is the key first step in creating your Action Plan.

There are two options—both equally effective—for creating input for your Action Plan:

1. The web-based RQ Assessment (Online Relational Intelligence test) referred to on this book's cover and featured in this chapter, which automatically provides objective tips and strategies for your Action Plan.

2. The Action Plan approach described in chapter 11 that does not require the RQ Assessment input. Therefore, if you are not at your computer, please skip ahead to the "Relational Insights" at the end of this chapter and proceed to chapter 11 so that you can continue with the Action Plan process.

RQ Assessment

Once you have identified your Fab 5, you can take the RQ Assessment. This tool will provide you with an insightful measurement of your *relational intelligence* for your five most important business relationships. While this assessment takes only about twenty to thirty minutes to complete, the resulting analysis and suggestions for advancing business relationships will have an *ongoing impact* on your ability to achieve the strategies in your Action Plan and business objectives.

Your RQ is calculated based on our analysis and weighting of the thirty-five most common behaviors experienced by thousands of business professionals. We have converted the analysis and weights to work within a 100-point scale, allowing you to easily understand the status of each of your own Fab 5.

Here are the instructions for calculating your RQ and developing your Action Plan:

1. Visit www.relationalcapitalgroup.com/tools/signup to create your free account. (If you have any questions or need any help, please contact us at info@relcapgroup.com.)

2. You will be asked to provide some basic profile information, including your name, e-mail address, a password of your choice, and the name of your company and industry. For the User Code field, enter the unique ID number found on the backside (underside) of your book's dust jacket. This unique

User Code needs to be entered in order to access the RQ Assessment.

3. After creating your account, follow the link to view your profile. From here, you can begin your RQ Assessment. You can access this assessment at any time using the links at the upper right-hand corner of the website.

4. You will enter the names of your Fab 5 (as shown in figure 10.1), along with the key performance objectives for each relationship, and then respond to questions that will ultimately connect you to the state of the relationship in terms of the criteria for each dimension and step on the Relational Ladder.

Figure 10.1: Example RQ Data Entry Screen

Step 1: Identify Your 5 Most Important Relationships and Related Goals

Enter your 5 most important business relationships and the relevant objectives/performance criteria that you will achieve by advancing these relationships. Please consider key existing or targeted future relationships in your industry and/or community that are closely tied to your objectives and business networking. (Full names or initials are acceptable. Five names are required to make your score meaningful.)

Relationship #1 [   ]
Why? [   ]

Relationship #2 [   ]
Why? [   ]

Relationship #3 [   ]
Why? [   ]

Relationship #4 [   ]
Why? [   ]

Relationship #5 [   ]
Why? [   ]

After you have answered all the questions in the assessment as accurately and authentically as possible, you will be asked to click a button to calculate your RQ. This will generate your personalized RQ Summary, a report which will give you detailed information about the status of each of your Fab 5 relationships and suggestions for your Action Plan.

Figure 10.2 shows an example of the initial part of the RQ Summary.

Figure 10.2: Example of First Part of RQ Summary

RQ Summary—Overview

Congratulations! You have successfully calculated your RQ. The RQ is a measure of both the strength and the level of your relational intelligence with your five most important business relationships. Your initial RQ provides you with a benchmark as you work to sustain and improve each business relationship.

This report displays:

- Your RQ score and range
- The distribution of your relationships among the Acquaintance, Professional Peer, and Respected Advisor dimensions
- The level within each dimension (the RQ Assessment uses three Acquaintance, three Professional Peer, and five Respected Advisor levels in order to smooth out overlapping client behaviors)
- Detailed suggestions on ways to improve each of your five most important business relationships

We encourage you to use the tips and suggestions [*Note*: This part of the report is provided later in this chapter to create your Action Plan and then follow through on your plan with your coach/manager].

Your RQ is **48.2**
Your RQ range is **35 to 76**
(Your RQ falls within this range for your combination of relationship dimensions.)

About the Distribution of Your Relationships

Our calculations indicate that you have:

2 Acquaintance Relationships

Most business relationships begin in this dimension and require relational capital investment to advance beyond a transactional relationship.

Figure 10.2: Example of First Part of RQ Summary (continued)

2 Professional Peer Relationships

Dimension where your client values you professionally and views you as a peer despite your role/level in the business relationship.

1 Respected Advisor Relationship

Highest dimension in the RQ process where your advice is sought on issues and decisions outside of the original business reason/issue that brought you together.

Your score indicates that you have a diverse set of relationships across the Acquaintance, Professional Peer, and Respected Advisor dimensions. This diversity is a healthy combination because it indicates your ability to advance important business relationships as well as your ongoing efforts to add new relationships to your network.

Your RQ range reveals the minimum and maximum scores for your combination of business relationships and their advancement. Subsequent RQ Assessments help you measure progress against your Action Plan strategies as you work to advance your most important business relationships.

The maximum RQ is 100.

However, it is likely that your score will fall below 100 as most participants have business relationships at varying levels when they complete the assessment. Keep in mind that the main objective is to continue to increase relational capital with every business contact. In fact, we will offer suggestions even for those rare occasions when participants score 100 on their RQ because maintaining even the highest level relationships requires ongoing commitment.

What's Next?

The RQ Summary gives you an in-depth, objective assessment of the level and strength of each relationship. In other words, it places the relationship in one of the three main dimensions — Acquaintance, Professional Peer, or Respected Advisor — and, within that dimension, rates the relationship on a point scale indicating where you are within the dimension. This tells you, for instance, the optimal time to begin to move out of the Professional Peer dimension into Respected Advisor status.

The RQ Summary also presents helpful tips, customized to your particular position in relation to each client, on how you could go about advancing the relationship to a higher level.

A great first step in understanding more about the important business relationships you shared through completing the RQ Assessment is to review each of the specific relationship assessments and suggestions for your Fab 5. An example of these follows.

RELATIONSHIP 1: PAUL JONES

Objective(s): Will directly influence 25% of my recurring business next year

Your relationship with **Paul Jones** is a **Respected Advisor—Level 2**.

Tips for improving this relationship:

- As you move up the Respected Advisor dimension with your integrity at a high level, you begin to realize returns on your relationship. Your client is willing to act as a referral or reference for you. Also, you should begin learning more about appropriate levels of your client's confidential information and be included in his planning processes.

- Continue to realize relational capital gains by:
  - Beginning to think about ways to offer help
  - Continuing to prepare for meetings and interactions, no "ad-libs"
  - Respecting your client's and his staff/team's time by focusing on the task/issue at hand
  - Following up on every commitment

RELATIONSHIP 2: FRANK SMITH

Objective(s): Close first sale opportunity with this client

Your relationship with **Frank Smith** is an **Acquaintance—Level 3**.

Tips for improving this relationship:

Because the opportunity to begin "investing in the relationship" is emerging, consider:

- Always preparing for meetings and interactions, no "ad-libs"
- Valuing both your client's and your own time
- Focusing on the task/issue at hand (connecting on the initial task/issue and bringing it to a successful conclusion supports moving up to the Professional Peer dimension)

RELATIONSHIP 3: GARY WILSON

Objective(s): Seek 2 referrals within this client's company in order to generate $50K in new business

Your relationship with **Gary Wilson** is a **Professional Peer—Level 2**.

Tips for improving this relationship:

As you move up within the Professional Peer dimension, you will begin learning more about your client's business goals, passions, and struggles. The client should also begin making and keeping some commitments to you. Consider the following to keep "securing the relationship":

- Continuing to sincerely inquire regarding your client's Relational GPS
- Listening closely and acknowledging your understanding
- Acknowledging your own goals and issues related to the topic
- Following up on every commitment

RELATIONSHIP 4: JOE BUYER

Objective(s): Grow this client's purchases by 15%

Your relationship with **Joe Buyer** is a **Professional Peer—Level 1**.

Tips for improving this relationship:

You have now moved beyond the Acquaintance dimension with your client and have begun the journey to take the relationship to the higher, Professional Peer dimension. You should begin experiencing more of a willingness to meet and work on additional opportunities with this client. Consider the following:

- Offering your own personal common ground when appropriate
- Inquiring into your client's additional goals, passions, and struggles
- Avoiding offering answers and solutions at this stage in the relationship

RELATIONSHIP 5: GREG CLOSER

Objective(s): Opportunity to collectively advance business with common clients

Your relationship with **Greg Closer** is an **Acquaintance—Level 2.**

Tips for improving this relationship:

You have developed some credibility by establishing common ground and now need to consider "securing the relationship" by:

- Sharing facts and not opinions on the issues and topics under discussion
- Listening closely to your contact and acknowledging your understanding
- Making routine commitments for follow-through (significant commitments are not appropriate or desired by your contact at this stage)

I would like to invite you to let the RQ Assessment become your personal secret weapon, your benchmark to regularly assess and improve the quality of your business relationships. Use it, and watch how the results of this process help drive the results of your business. Best of luck!

Only by measuring can we truly manage and advance.

RELATIONAL INSIGHTS

☑ The RQ Assessment is an effective way to measure the value of your most important business relationships.

☑ RQ tips and suggestions contribute to the development of your Action Plan.

☑ Once you establish a baseline score for your Fab 5, you can then gauge where you stand on the Relational Ladder and measure your progress against your Action Plan by taking additional RQ Assessments.

Chapter 11

Creating and Sustaining
Your Action Plan

*Plans are only good intentions unless they immediately degenerate
into hard work.*
—Peter Drucker

I mentioned earlier that "goals are just dreams until we write them down." In that context, I asked you to reflect on your objectives for the next twelve months and then write down the five most important business relationships you need to advance to achieve these objectives. Now that your "dreams" are written, a plan and strategies are required to fulfill them. This chapter is about creating an Action Plan for your Fab 5 and then starting immediately to implement your plan.

Action Plan

If you did not take the RQ Assessment in the last chapter, you can still develop input to your Action Plan because you have read through all the chapters explaining the principle of worthy intent and the essential qualities of credibility, integrity, and authenticity, and you understand the Relational Ladder and the meaning of being an Acquaintance, a Professional Peer, or a Respected Advisor. You also have a clear sense of what these dimensions imply and therefore a more realistic sense of where you stand in your business relationships.

Appendix A has a sample Action Plan template. Download an electronic version at www.relationalcapitalgroup.com/actionplan. Please use this Action Plan template and follow the process in this chapter whether you generated an RQ Summary in chapter 10 or you plan to develop your Action Plan without that input. Complete each item as suggested in the list that follows so that you can create strategies and specific steps to advance each business relationship in order to achieve your key performance objectives.

1. Enter your Important Business Relationship
2. Quantify "Why" with the contribution to your quota and other performance criteria
3. Think about each of your Fab 5 relationships, and with a commitment to yourself to be as authentic as you can, determine and check off whether each relationship is an Acquaintance, Professional Peer, or Respected Advisor. If you used the RQ Assessment, revisit the results and consider making any changes to the dimensions suggested. Following is an example of these first three steps.

IMPORTANT BUSINESS RELATIONSHIP: PAUL JONES

Why? (Contribution to quotas and other performance criteria)

Will directly influence 25% of my recurring business next year

Relational Ladder dimension (check one):

☐ Acquaintance   ☐ Professional Peer   ☑ Respected Advisor

Relational Ladder Strategies

Figure 11.1 provides a targeted summary of twenty specific strategies for the five steps and dimensions of the Relational Ladder that my clients use to create their Action Plans. The first time through an Action Plan can be challenging, so please consider using or expanding on these suggestions.

I applied some of the suggestions listed in Figure 11.1 to complete the following Action Plan for the business relationship of Paul Jones, as shown in the following example. Note that the Action Plan template that you can download also includes a section to record additional commitments and any noteworthy information as you activate your plan. Please use these sections as needed to continue advancing your important business relationship.

IMPORTANT BUSINESS RELATIONSHIP: PAUL JONES

Why? (Contribution to quotas and other performance criteria)

Will directly influence 25% of my recurring business next year

Relational Ladder dimension (check one):

☐ Acquaintance   ☐ Professional Peer   ☑ Respected Advisor

Strategy to move up the Relational Ladder:

Offer help

Learn more about how our new service offering can support Paul's objectives

Refer a colleague who can help Paul with a particular issue

Offer some ideas to help Paul select a college for his daughter

Current commitments: Review and sign off on Paul's changes to our agreement

Time frame: By month's end

Date completed: June 28th

Figure 11.1: Relational Ladder Strategies

1. Establishing Common Ground: Launch the Relationship	
• Create person-to-person connections • Ask about your client's goals and aspirations	• Understand your client's business issues • Resist the urge to offer answers and solutions
2. Displaying Integrity and Trust: Secure the Relationship	
• Be honest about issues • Share facts and not opinions	• Listen, take notes, and document decisions • Always follow up on all commitments
3. Using Time Purposefully: Invest in the Relationship	
• Value your client's time • Always prepare for meetings and interactions	• Value your own time • Be in the moment
4. Offering Help: Share Relational Equity	
• Focus on being yourself • Understand your client's goals, passions, and struggles	• Offer ideas aligned with your client's goals, passions, and struggles • Treat each challenge as unique
5. Asking for Help: Realize Significant Returns on Your Relationship Investment	
• Focus on being yourself • Seek to influence rather than direct decisions	• Be able to say, "I don't know!" and ask for help • Seek help with your own goals, passions, and struggles

Actualizing Your Plan—A Continuous Process

In my experience, it's important to view both the RQ Assessment and the Action Plan as continual works in progress, just like your relationships themselves. Together, they provide a snapshot of where you are in your Fab 5 business relationships at any given time. While it's highly valuable to get this snapshot and understand what it says about how you are advancing these relationships, it's also important to view this information as a starting point, a personal agenda for change. Using the RQ Assessment as a basis to develop your Action Plan, you will record over time how you approach the task of improving each relationship and moving it further up the Relational Ladder.

Then, at a point when you feel you have accomplished significant progress with your Fab 5, it's time to complete the RQ Assessment all over again. Only by repeating this process can you have an idea of how far you've actually come. The new results will either confirm your feeling of progress, giving you hard evidence to validate the improvements made, or give you information to guide you in your continued efforts.

Figure 11.2 shows the perpetual nature of the steps involved in creating your Action Plan. Each cycle of assessment, action planning, and measuring improvements is an opportunity to renew your commitment to putting into practice the principle of worthy intent and topics discussed in all the previous chapters—starting

Figure 11.2: Action Plan Cycle

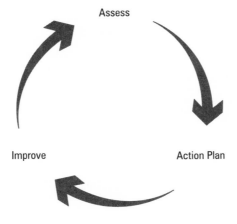

Assess

Action Plan

Improve

with credibility, integrity, and authenticity. Everything else flows from these; nothing happens without them.

Relational Reinforcers

My hope is that now that you've almost completed *Business Relationships That Last* you are very enthusiastic and energized to put this new learning into action with all of your business relationships. The challenge you face is to take your energy and the ideas you learned and get sustained behavioral change from them. Adults need at least seven touch points with new information to really make it part of their approach to advancing business relationships.

I can tell you from my own experience that after reading a book or attending a seminar, if I don't apply what I've learned right away, I rarely develop those intended skills and behaviors. With that in mind, I've created some simple-to-use relational reinforcer exercises that will help you further internalize what you've learned from this book and incorporate it into your daily routine so you can fulfill your Action Plan. By making a commitment to yourself to do so, you will be on the path to consistently advance your relationships up the Relational Ladder.

The relational reinforcer exercises that follow are a subset of the tools that I use with clients. (These can be found in the Knowledge Center at www.relationalcapitalgroup.com.) I am continuously adding new ideas and tools like these based on client feedback, so please visit the Knowledge Center as often as you can.

Internalizing one reinforcer leads to your ongoing usage of it and then the ability to move on to the next reinforcer. With each exercise you make your own, you are that much closer to achieving sustained relational fluency.

Reinforcer #1: Being in the Moment

Max was very skilled at listening and remembering. This allowed him to develop outstanding business relationships and superior performance. Here's a checklist of "reinforcer" behaviors to help you immediately focus on the client at hand and turn listening and remembering into relational attributes that your client identifies with you:

☐ Clarify meeting expectations — attendees, time frame, purpose — preferably in advance.

☐ Review any noteworthy business and relational information from a previous meeting. For example, your client's firm just announced an acquisition, or your client recently had a baby; how could either event impact project schedules and your work with the client?

☐ Set a goal of seeking to learn more about your client's Relational GPS — goals, passions, and struggles — during your next meeting. For example, during your next client meeting discuss a solution and also seek to learn about one additional goal, passion, or struggle.

☐ Resist the urge to offer solutions and answers too early in the process.

Exercise

Practice this relational reinforcer by applying it to each of your next five client interactions.

Relational Fluency Indicators

You will have internalized this reinforcer when you:

• Review or mentally consider this checklist prior to all client interactions.

• Consider this behavior as required rather than optional.

Reinforcer #2: Overcoming Relational Blockers

You read in chapter 3 about six categories of relational blockers that get in the way of outstanding business relationships:

- Feature and Function Obsession
- Your Perpetual Audition
- BlackBerry Addiction Disorder
- Busyness
- Instant Gratification Is Not Fast Enough
- Quality Versus Quantity of Relationships

Exercise

1. Reflect on one of your business relationships that has stalled. Identify which behaviors have blocked your ability to advance that particular relationship.

2. Repeat this with two other business relationships.

3. Create a strategy to overcome each blocker. For example, avoid feature and function discussions, and focus instead on asking sincere, credible questions to demonstrate your competence.

Relational Fluency Indicators

You will have internalized this reinforcer when you:

- Can identify which relational blocker is holding you back from advancing a business relationship.
- Demonstrate that you have overcome the relational blocker by having a client share more of his or her Relational GPS with you.

Reinforcer #3: Creating Relational Attributes

Max was able to translate his transactional activities, such as on-time arrivals and an impeccable taxicab, into relational attributes, like respecting riders' needs and time, that distinguished him with his riders and led to outstanding business relationships and repeat business.

Exercise

1. Complete the following statement by naming the three relational attributes you believe that your clients attach to you during your interactions with them:

   "My clients work with me because . . ."

2. Identify the specific client behaviors you can cite to support your responses.

Relational Fluency Indicators

You will have internalized this reinforcer when you:

- Receive unsolicited input from your clients about these specific attributes.
- Notice that your client begins to share more aspects of his or her Relational GPS when you meet.

Reinforcer #4: Commitments

We display our integrity, create relational capital, and advance our business relationships when we deliver on the commitments we make to our clients. Because we make many commitments to multiple clients each week, this reinforcer is designed to help you develop clear, concise commitments (see the example below). Most CRM processes have the capability to record and update your client commitments and then to communicate with the client that you have delivered. You can adapt this format to work with almost any CRM process.

Exercise

Download the Client Commitments template at www.relational capitalgroup.com/commitments. Following is an example.

CLIENT COMMITMENT

Commitment: As agreed, deliver revised project proposal to client's CEO

Time frame: 11/12

Date completed: 11/9

Client update: Notified client of closure on this commitment while she was out of town

Relational Fluency Indicators

You will have internalized this reinforcer when you:

- Track and follow through consistently on all open promises to your clients and share the results of previous commitments.

- Can report that clients continue to ask you to make commitments around new opportunities.

Reinforcer #5: Doing Business on a Handshake

Business has become very complicated both from a documentation standpoint and from a legal perspective. However, within every business relationship there are opportunities to deliver on commitments or to take steps to advance the relationship with a handshake. This helps you display your integrity and trust and makes it easier for your client to do business with you.

Exercise

Think about three existing client opportunities, and for each one, develop a way to deliver on commitments or other aspects of working together with a handshake.

Relational Fluency Indicators

You will have internalized this reinforcer when you:

- Hear a client mention how easy it is to do business together.
- Observe that your client begins to suggest handshake opportunities for you as well.

Reinforcer #6: Plan Your Next Client Meeting

Chapter 7 covered how Professional Peers and Respected Advisors seek to use their clients' time purposefully when working together. One way to exhibit that is through planning for effective meetings. POP—Purpose, Outcomes, and Process—represents three repeatable steps for planning and then collaborating around a client meeting. Download a POP template at www.relationalcapital group.com/POP and try the following exercise:

Exercise

Plan your next client meeting using POP. Forward it to your client and ask for his or her upgrades.

Relational Fluency Indicators

You will have internalized this reinforcer when you:

- Make POP a routine planning aspect of every meeting.
- Receive compliments from your clients for taking such great care with your interactions.

Reinforcer #7: Referrals — Blind Dating

Here's an insightful way to think about referrals. Reflect on one of your Respected Advisor or Professional Peer relationships: think about how you have demonstrated credibility, integrity, and authenticity, and where you are on the Relational Ladder.

1. If you had asked for this client's help with a referral, what would you hope the client would say about you when he makes the referral?

2. What could you do to ensure that the client would say what you desired?

Exercise

When you want to ask for a referral, walk through these steps to determine which type of referral you should seek:

1. Think of the attributes that your client has ascribed to you.

2. Based on these attributes, determine whether you should seek a passive or a direct referral.

3. Develop a passive referral.

4. Develop a direct referral.

Relational Fluency Indicators

You will have internalized this reinforcer when you:

- Are comfortable asking for referrals on at least a quarterly basis in Professional Peer and Respected Advisor relationships.

- Begin to receive unsolicited referrals from your Respected Advisor clients.

Automating Your Action Plan

Advancing client relationships requires a unique blend of people, process, and technology. I mentioned earlier in this book that only 24 percent of companies formally *track* the relational aspects of their client and prospect interactions within their CRM processes. I also shared that less than 5 percent actually focus on *advancing* business relationships as a strategy for achieving their forecasts and quotas. I recently learned how one of my clients embedded the Relational Ladder into its CRM/sales work-flow processes because the company wanted to transform its focus on advancing business relationships into a repeatable approach for internal use as well as client use.

That client is actually a sales work-flow automation company committed to making sure that the new relational skills we shared with them translated to Action Plans and that those Action Plans turned into revenue. The challenge with any new client-facing method or process is rapid deployment and adoption of the new skills and activities throughout the client-facing team in order to drive adoption. I learned that they were using their own web-based technology to automate various aspects of the Relational Ladder. They are now capable of providing their client-facing professionals with appropriate selling aids at the proper stage in the sales cycle, identify and understand buyers' Relational GPS, and translate relationship development into discreet selling activities.

This is a great example of how you can automate your Action Plan within you own CRM process.

Planning our actions will lead to greater performance only when we actually become actionable.

RELATIONAL INSIGHTS

☑ Identifying your Fab 5—the five most important business relationships connected to your key performance objectives—is the first step in developing your Action Plan.

☑ Classifying each relationship as an Acquaintance, a Professional Peer, or a Respected Advisor leads to action planning strategies for each relationship.

☑ Delivering on your commitments to advance your business relationships turns your strategies into action.

☑ Continuous assessment of each relationship eliminates the chance of sliding back down the Relational Ladder.

Chapter 12

Relational Capital Gains

Every little thing has a big purpose.
—Max

Moving up the Relational Ladder is a dynamic process by which you achieve progressively higher levels of relational capital with your clients. You do this by having worthy intent and re-appreciating and demonstrating the qualities of relational capital — credibility, integrity, and authenticity — that begin to intensify as they converge and culminate in an outstanding business relationship.

This convergence occurs throughout the process and results in what I've come to regard as relational capital gains — *that is,* dynamic increases in reserves of trust and goodwill and the eventual attainment of Professional Peer and Respected Advisor status for your business relationships.

Relational capital gains lead to long-term, sustainable business relationships that last. Here is an informal, partial list of common behaviors and interactions that indicate you are generally building significant relational capital with your business contacts and clients. The more of these you can identify as being present in your business relationships, the more likely it is that you are already experiencing the benefits of creating relational capital.

RELATIONAL CAPITAL GAINS

☑ You are able to ask for help from colleagues and clients.

☑ Business contacts are willing to recommend you on a regular basis to their peers.

☑ People from all levels in your organization take you into their confidence and seek your help and input.

☑ Clients share confidences with you and invite you into their planning processes.

☑ Your decisions that turn into mistakes are viewed as opportunities rather than failures.

☑ Open and honest conversations with your manager do not lead to career risk.

☑ Your clients are confident that their decisions to buy at your higher price are right due to their belief in the distinctive value of your relationship.

☑ You continue to be a valued reference for people as they move through their own career opportunities.

☑ You view negative input from your clients as an opportunity to strengthen the relationship.

☑ Your clients provide early warning signs for potential issues so you are not blindsided.

☑ You are comfortable referring business solutions that you cannot effectively provide.

☑ Your advice is often sought on issues and decisions not directly related to the original business issue that brought you together.

If you reflect for a moment on your own client experiences, you will likely be able to add your own examples of relational capital gains to this list. Creating these gains in business adds critical value in these important ways:

- High-performing relationships are better equipped to weather inevitable business downturns and other uncontrollable factors.

- Relational capital transforms a business environment from a focus on transactions and tactical accomplishments to a focus on the value each party brings to the relationship.

- Relational capital helps client-facing professionals transcend the sense of urgency and panic that permeates much of today's global commerce. Both parties are able to operate on a higher plain, working as partners who are better able to identify each other's Relational GPS—and achieve real productivity for each other.

The stronger the relational capital gains, the easier it is to compensate for imbalances in the science (hard skills) and art (soft skills) in the process. This, in turn, contributes to improved performance and reinforces the quality of the relationship. By the way, work and life are just a lot more enjoyable, too!

How better to demonstrate relational capital gains and their contribution to real business performance than to share a letter that a friend forwarded to me about one of his client-facing professionals?

Dear Greg,

I thought you might like some feedback regarding my experience in dealing with Ronald, your Director of Marketing, because you should be aware that you have someone on your team who is . . . well . . . a bit odd. We deal with people and companies across the country and around the world, and I must say that Ronald is somewhat "unique."

- *He is courteous and professional.*
- *He returns phone calls and e-mails [almost immediately].*
- *He is detail oriented.*
- *He actually follows through and does what he says he will do.*

In today's business environment in which so many people seem to be aloof and constantly "too busy," Ronald is truly the odd man out. Obviously, my note is tongue-in-cheek, but the point is that Ronald is a great guy to work with, and his professionalism and follow-through are wonderfully refreshing. Also, he is excellent at what he does: for instance, he got me to agree to a deal that, at first, I thought would never fly. This deal ultimately resulted in more than 100 events and 150,000 participants, allowing us to make our numbers for the year.

If you can find more like him, then you should grab them.

Yours,

Phil

After reading this letter, do you think this client will ever want to do business with anyone else?

Rounding Down

One critical point to keep in mind about the three dimensions of the Relational Ladder is that they are only real if they are two-way. If you believe that you are a Professional Peer with someone, but you observe that she still treats you as if you were in a subservient position, then you are still in the Acquaintance dimension. If you feel you have become a Respected Advisor to a client, that you have given him lots of valuable advice, but he continues to work only within the scope of current business opportunities, then you are more likely a Professional Peer. In essence, you need to "round down" your evaluation if your client's behaviors are not aligned with yours. (Appendix B, "Relational Capital Lite," provides a fast and easy way to get some perspective on how your client views you.)

Relational capital is all about building and maintaining mutual trust and respect, starting — as every single relationship does — in the Acquaintance dimension. We have to be realistic in how we assess the quality and depth of each relationship or else we may be fooling ourselves. By rounding down, you eliminate the chance for a relational superiority complex to mask where you really stand no matter what dimension you have established in each of your business relationships.

While you might set the goal of being in the Respected Advisor dimension with every business contact you make, it's unlikely you'll ever achieve this across the board. There will always be contacts with whom you enjoy Professional Peer status and others with whom you might never move beyond being in the Acquaintance dimension. Keep in mind that you have some level of relational capital with everyone you do business with. Given the impact that relationships can have on your performance, consider striving to upgrade each relationship regardless of how the person views you or your role.

The Secret to Success

Client-facing professionals work in a world where the pace of technology and innovation leads to rapid duplication and commoditization and, therefore, razor-thin margins for error when working with clients. I mentioned previously that, as client-facing professionals, we all have quotas and business objectives, but we rarely take into account a strategy for the people and relationships required to achieve these objectives. But by focusing on creating relational capital and consciously connecting our performance objectives to the advancement of our business relationships, we have given ourselves a strategy to succeed in this challenging business environment.

At this point in reading *Business Relationships That Last* you

- Understand the principle of worthy intent
- Have learned to re-appreciate the essential qualities of credibility, integrity, and authenticity
- Realize that your ability to deliver on these essential qualities leads to the relational attributes assigned to you by your clients
- Can use the 5 Steps to Transform Contacts into High-Performing Relationships of the Relational Ladder
- Understand that each client's Relational GPS — goals, passions, and struggles — is your road map to ascend the Relational Ladder and attain business relationships that last (see figure 12.1).
- Have identified your Fab 5, the five most important business relationships to help you make your quota and other performance objectives
- Can calculate your relational intelligence (RQ) for your Fab 5

- Have completed your first Action Plan
- Understand that many business leaders and client-facing professionals have become successful due to a focus on creating relational capital with every business contact
- Have many new insights and new skills for sustained behavioral change to distinguish yourself and make your business pursuits more prosperous and enjoyable

You have now created enough relational capital gains to move up the Relational Ladder. You have closed the relational gap that

Figure 12.1: Relational Ladder—Business Relationships That Last

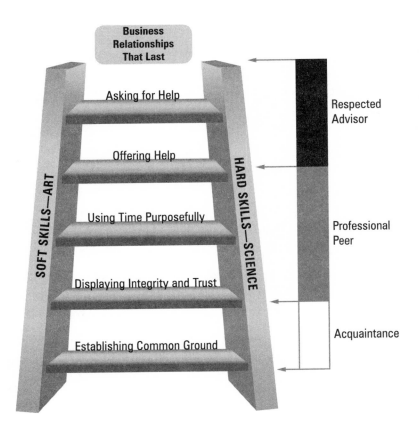

exists when client-facing professionals lack strategies to advance the relationships required to achieve their objectives. You no longer need to take chances or rely on "magic" to develop outstanding business relationships.

One Final Tribute to Max

One of the most common questions clients ask toward the end of my workshops is, "Where is Max today?" To answer this question I'd like to close this book with one more reflection on my great friend and Respected Advisor.

Max was a remarkable human being, and it has been my pleasure and honor to share our friendship throughout this book. No wonder he had such a successful career and — even better — such a successful life. Who wouldn't want to do business with someone so genuine, someone who had such a strong sense of service to others? His business performance was of the type we all want and hope we can offer. As a client-facing professional, think about the following elements of Max's approach that helped him deliver this great performance:

- **Customer loyalty**: Max's friends needed to schedule a ride with him three to four weeks in advance. Everyone wanted to travel with him, and we were genuinely disappointed when he was booked.

- **Increased revenue per trip**: While the fare was regulated, I always tipped Max more than I usually tipped other drivers, and I suspect his other friends did as well.

- **Recurring business**: Max's "pipeline" was full and easy to forecast month after month because of repeat business from his friends.

Competitor-proof: I never thought about taking a different driver or taxi service.

Respected Advisor: Max attained the highest relational capital gains with everyone from CEOs to client-facing professionals like me.

Those who spent time with Max found that he would listen enthusiastically to whatever they wanted to talk about, finding it fresh and fascinating. Max never marginalized any person or topic. The interests of his fares became the interests of his friends, to which he became committed and showed his worthy intent. Max also never patronized anyone. You never had the feeling he was trying to get something from you or his interaction with you. He was totally present, totally in the moment.

In fact, you had the feeling he *already had* everything he wanted or needed — the enjoyment he found in life and in each one of his friendships. Figure 12.2 depicts just some of the ways in which Max built business relationships that last.

Max passed away much too soon in our relationship, and I suspect a lot of other people feel the same way. He had lived his life in service to his family and friends, and that is how he is remembered and appreciated. To me he was a special friend who took joy in making the ordinary unique and in helping me understand the importance of applying common principles in powerful new ways. His life and legacy have made my life a better one and will continue to do so for a long time to come.

Figure 12.2: Relational Insights from Max

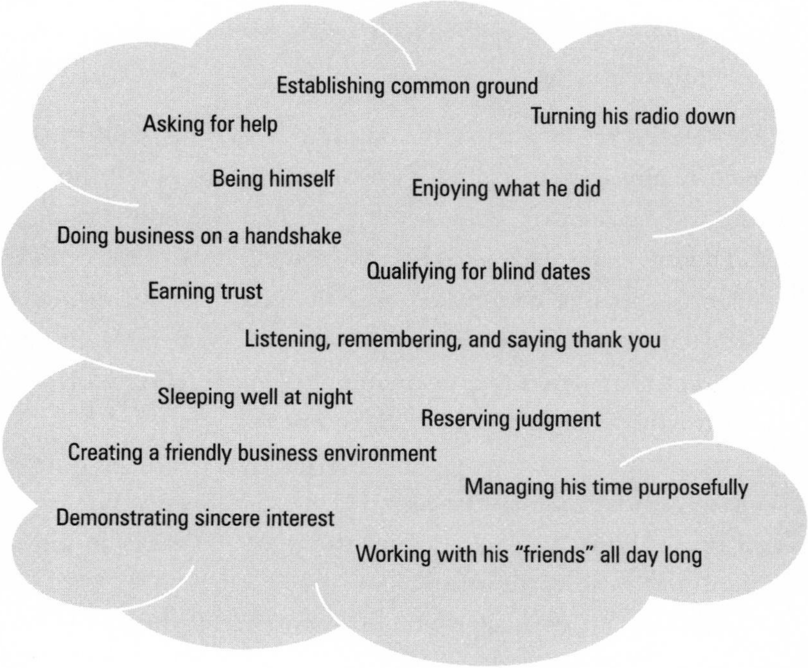

Establishing common ground

Asking for help

Turning his radio down

Being himself

Enjoying what he did

Doing business on a handshake

Qualifying for blind dates

Earning trust

Listening, remembering, and saying thank you

Sleeping well at night

Reserving judgment

Creating a friendly business environment

Managing his time purposefully

Demonstrating sincere interest

Working with his "friends" all day long

Appendix A

Action Plan

Here's the sample Action Plan template referred to in chapter 11 (see figure A.1). Go to www.relationalcapitalgroup.com/actionplan to download the full template in order to complete your Action Plan for advancing your Fab 5—your five most important business relationships—and connecting them to your objectives for the next twelve months.

When completing your Action Plan, remember to

- Select an important business relationship that will help you achieve your quota
- Be specific and quantify "why" you are including this business relationship—for example, this relationship will contribute 15 percent toward this year's quota

- Check off a Relational Ladder dimension to guide your strategy
- Develop a strategy to advance your business relationship based on the dimension selected and your new learning from this book
- Keep track of your commitments
- Add noteworthy information you have learned

Note: Using the Action Plan template, complete a strategy for each of your Fab 5. Review and update your Action Plan weekly.

Figure A.1: Sample Action Plan Template

Important Business Relationship: _____

Why?
(Contribution to quotas and other performance criteria)

_____

_____

_____

Relational Ladder dimension (check one):

_____ Acquaintance _____ Professional Peer _____ Respected Advisor

Strategy to move up the Relational Ladder:

_____

_____

_____

Commitment: _____

_____

_____

Time frame:

Date completed:

Client updated: _____

_____

Relational GPS:

Goals: _____

Passions: _____

Struggles: _____

Appendix B

Relational Capital Lite

Unlike the RQ Assessment, the Relational Capital Lite (as shown in figure B.1) is a nonscientific way for you to get a glimpse of how your clients see and attach attributes to you as you are developing your business relationships with each of them.

Relational Capital Lite prompts you to be intellectually honest about your development of the essential qualities — credibility, integrity, and authenticity — in a business relationship. Relational Capital Lite can be used at any time for a quick understanding of where you stand.

Go to www.relationalcapitalgroup.com/rclite to download a copy of the Relational Capital Lite template, and then complete it to see where you stand in your business relationships.

Figure B.1: Relational Capital Lite

Relational Capital Lite

How I Believe My Client Views Me

1. Client's Name/Initials: _____

2. ## Score Yourself from 1 to 3 Points
   1 = low, 2 = medium, and 3 = high

Quality		Score
Credibility	My client finds me to be "believable."	☐
	I inspire confidence during our interactions with my "knowledge and capabilities."	☐
Integrity	My client sees me as "trustworthy" and having "high ethics."	☐
	I live up to my "promises."	☐
Authenticity	My client views me as "genuine" and "open."	☐
	I am "transparent" in my communications.	☐
	Total	☐

3. Relational Capital Lite Interpretation

Circle the range that corresponds with the total from step two. Provide a brief rationale for the rating.

Your Total	Your Rationale
14–18: I have excellent Relational Capital with my client.	
9–13: I have good Relational Capital but need to strengthen one area.	
4–8: I have weak Relational Capital in many areas; I need to focus on the weakest areas first.	
0–3: I have NO Relational Capital with my client; I need to assess whether this is due to my client's lack of really knowing me or actual behaviors I have exhibited.	

4. Next Steps

Take a few minutes to reflect on your Relational Capital Lite score and determine what steps you can take, based on what you've learned from this book, to include in your Action Plan.

1. _____

_____

2. _____

_____

3. _____

_____

 **The Relational Capital Group**

Services Available

My firm, The Relational Capital Group, helps organizations identify, assess, and advance the key relationships that most impact current and future business performance. Organizations adopting our Relational Ladder™ process create key performance advantages leading to improved relationship effectiveness, profitability and sustainability in the global marketplace. We do this in the following ways:

- Keynote talks for conferences and corporate events

- Assessments

- Workshops

- Custom tailored programs

Custom Tailored Programs Include:

- Collaboration with executives to develop the best Relational Capital strategy in support of their brand and objectives;

- Measurement of the actual value of each professional's business relationships through RQ™—our web-based assessment tool;

- Implementation of our repeatable approach to increase tracking and visibility;

- Generation of management level reports that provide data on where key relationships stand and progress against objectives;

- Accountability and throughput are ensured through our executive coaches who are executives currently working in industry.

We tailor each of our programs and solutions so they can be used as a stand alone or incorporated into any CRM or contact management system that your organization is using. Here are a few examples of the results that we've proudly helped our clients achieve:

A. National sales team shortened its sales cycle by 22% in 6 months;

B. Account management team increased its key account penetration rate by 34% in one fiscal year;

C. Leadership team implemented our methodology organization-wide leading to 28% improvement in customer retention.

For further information on these programs and offerings contact **programs@relcapgroup.com**.

Visit our Knowledge Center at www.relcapgroup.com for:

- Complementary information

- Relational capital development tools

- Case studies

The Relational Capital Group

Additional Titles from Ed Wallace

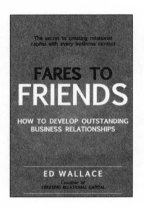

Fares to Friends

How to Develop Outstanding Business Relationships

By Ed Wallace

"Ed Wallace is a proven master of the art of the successful business relationship."
—Jeff Westphal, President & CEO Vertex, Inc.

ISBN 978-1-4243-3102-4

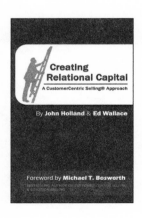

Creating Relational Capital

A CustomerCentric Selling® Approach

By John Holland and Ed Wallace
Forward by Michael T. Bosworth

"Creating Relational Capital is a gem!"
—Gerhard Gschwandtner, Founder & CEO,
Selling Power Magazine

ISBN 978-1-60461-132-8